Praise for *School Improvement: 9 Systemic Processes to Raise Achievement*

All of our achievement scores have gone up. Students who come from poverty are closing the achievement gap. Not only are they catching up with their peers, but as all our test scores go up exponentially, they are right there with them.

—Dr. Wynona Winn, Superintendent, 2000–07, Hutc'... ʌls, KS

The concepts from Framework were taught to many of our fac... last spring. Those concepts, combined with increased Student Services ... gram directors, community outreach, faculty involvement, and a lot of hard ... ʌed in our annual attrition rate going from 6% to 4.3% last year.

—Ada Gerard, Campus President, Heald College, Rancho Cordova, CA

Ruby's work is about systems, and these systems help you get to the root causes, and, to me, I thought that was promising, whether you're talking about reforming a school or you're talking about reforming a community. It gave us that hope.

—Wendell Waukau, Superintendent, Menominee Indian School District, Neopit, WI

We received our state test scores, and our students who were at 30% in literacy are now at 50%, which is a 20-point gain in a year.

—Lenisha Broadway, Principal, Ridgeroad Middle Charter School, North Little Rock, AR

Any district would benefit from being involved with the strategies and techniques that have been shared.

Ridgeroad Middle Charter School
- *Seventh grade—Math proficiency increased by 18%*
- *Eighth grade—Math proficiency increased by 13%*

—Kristie Ratliff, Director of School Improvement and Professional Development, North Little Rock, AR

The plan and label strategies have helped [students] a great deal—to slow down, to think through the problem that they need to solve, to better communicate their ideas on paper, and just to help them understand their thinking a lot better.

–Susan Tieman, Third-Grade and ESL Teacher, Southwick Elementary, Fort Wayne, IN

The time and content grids caused our teachers to work together and begin to look at what they're teaching and how they are timing it over 12 weeks of classes.

–Dr. Sue Neat, Principal, Blackford HS, Blackford, IN

School Improvement

Systemic Processes to Raise Achievement

Creating Sustainable Excellence

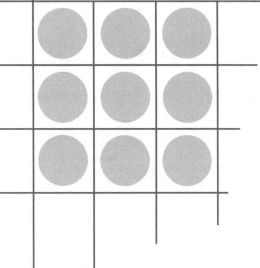

School Improvement: 9 Systemic Processes to Raise Achievement
Ruby K. Payne and Donna S. Magee
165 pp.
References pp. 153–154

© 2010 by aha! Process, Inc.
Published by aha! Process, Inc.

aha! Process, Inc.
P.O. Box 727
Highlands, TX 77562-0727
(800) 424-9484 ■ (281) 426-5300
Fax: (281) 426-5600
Website: www.ahaprocess.com

ISBN 13: 978-1-934583-44-9
ISBN 10: 1-934583-44-8

Copy editing by Dan Shenk
Book design by Paula Nicolella
Cover design by Naylor Design

Printed in the United States of America

School Improvement

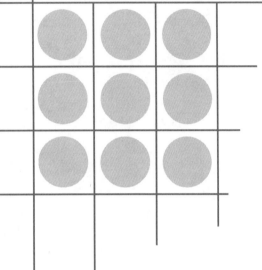

9

Systemic Processes to Raise Achievement

Creating Sustainable Excellence

Ruby K. Payne, Ph.D., and
Donna S. Magee, Ed.D.

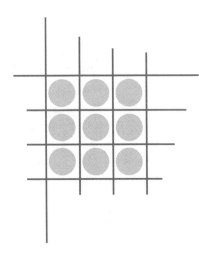

Acknowledgments

We gratefully acknowledge the contributions of the hundreds of teachers and administrators across the United States with whom we have been privileged to work to implement this model. Your efforts with students have made an incalculable difference.

We also acknowledge the work of all aha! Process, Inc., consultants who have provided training and technical assistance at these sites. We thank particularly Kim Ellis, Shelley Rex, Alecia Chapman, and Susie Spurgeon who assisted us in these revisions; Shelley also provided us with a wonderful gift of systematic thinking in helping develop the numerous Administrator Checklists.

We would be remiss if we failed to also acknowledge Dan Shenk, our editor; Paula Nicolella, our desktop publisher; Peggy Conrad, our vice president of Publications; and Dan Magee, who has always believed in and valued Ruby's work and has been a continuous support to Donna.

We wish you the best in your work!

Ruby Payne and Donna Magee

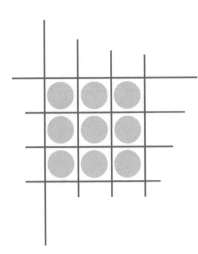

Table of Contents

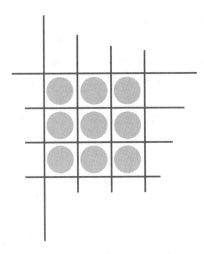

Introduction

Teacher-friendly. Collegial. Highly collaborative. Simpler processes that take less time and money.

These are all phrases that can be applied to the aha! Process School Improvement Model for Low-Performing Schools. As more and more schools face the consequences of not making the required growth in student achievement, a simpler yet comprehensive model is required. The work of Dr. Ruby K. Payne and her colleagues provides such a model, which has been used for nearly a decade. Results have shown that when the model is implemented with fidelity, student achievement increases and achievement gaps have even been narrowed at some sites.

The Model

Nine processes comprise the model for high-poverty schools. Each process has specific classroom applications aligned to the process that can be monitored by the school leader. The result is artifacts that reflect the processes, along with applications that extend strategies into the classroom.

The processes apply to all levels of schools, beginning with 4-year-olds and continuing through Grade 12. These processes can be taught to teachers in two-hour increments of time after the foundational workshops, A Framework for Understanding Poverty and Research-Based Strategies, are taught. Key understandings are included in Framework and Research-Based Strategies that are essential to success with the model. An optional but important training that schools may wish to consider is Meeting AYP with Six Simple Processes. While many of the nine processes are included in this training, the pace at which the processes can be implemented can be increased with this additional training. The nine processes that actually comprise the model are:

1. Gridding student data
2. Developing time and content grids, based on the standards and students' needs
3. Understanding assessment context, state assessment glossary, academic vocabulary, and the assessment blueprint
4. Developing 10-question tests that measure students' progress against the standards for the first semester
5. Identifying interventions based on analysis of 10-question tests and analyzing grade distribution or failure/passing rate
6. Understanding content comprehension and incorporating processes, step sheets, planning, and mental models into lessons; response to intervention also is addressed in this step

7. Developing 10-question tests for the second semester
8. Calibrating curriculum and completing artifact analyses using rubrics
9. Reviewing adult voice, putting students in charge of their own learning, and relational learning for students, including technology integration

Because these processes provide scaffolding for instruction, they are deliberately designed for delivery in the order outlined. The gridding of data identified as the first process is a mandatory step that must be completed by teachers when working with the aha! Process model. We realize that districts and schools have a great deal of data available to them and may have a process in place to disaggregate data, but our experience has been that unless the teachers themselves work through this first process, they seldom truly understand the implications of the data and the needs of the students with whom they are working. Many are not comfortable analyzing data and knowing how to use it effectively. They can be described as "data rich, but information poor" (Ronka, Lachat, Slaughter, & Meltzer, 2008, 2009).

As you work through the processes, you also will find that teachers are being asked to work in learning communities, to share best practices, and to support and work with one another. The professional dialog that occurs during these sessions can profoundly shape the culture of a building and the relationships of the adults who work together in it.

It is our hope that the model will inspire you in your process of change, that you will adapt it for your needs, and that you will focus on continuous improvement as you work with the strategies and refine and improve on them over the years.

Finally, this workbook is designed for use in a workshop setting. It is not intended to be a "stand alone" but to provide a reference tool for you after you complete the workshop.

School Improvement Model

	Process	Classroom Application
2 hours	Data analysis	Math—problem-solving model ELA—nonfiction reading strategy and open-response strategy Share examples of walk-throughs
2 hours	Assigning time, aligning instruction *	Bellwork
2 hours	Assessment context, state assessment glossary, academic vocabulary, assessment blueprint	Word wall, vocabulary sketching (mental models) (Consultant needs time scheduled with principal to review assessment blueprint)
2 hours	Ten-question tests—first semester: reading, writing, math	Examples of mental models
2 hours	Interventions, data analysis, grade distribution, failure rate	Resource analysis and interventions
2 hours	Content comprehension—processes, step sheets, planning, RTI, specific mental models	Research-based strategies and targeted interventions using intervention form
2 hours	Ten-question tests—second semester: reading, writing, math	Question making
2 hours	Curriculum calibration, artifacts analysis, rubrics	Rubrics: ELA teachers teach writing rubric and open-response rubric to entire staff
2 hours	Voice, putting students in charge of their own learning, relational learning	Data conferencing with students Monitor for use of adult voice in classroom Monitor for examples of relational learning

* Needs to be done for each content area

Foundational Workshops
A Framework for Understanding Poverty
Research-Based Strategies

Additional Offerings
- Curriculum alignment, beyond the development of the time and content grids
- Observation days
- Follow-up with new teachers with the consultant (use certified trainer for foundational trainings)

Required Texts
A Framework for Understanding Poverty
Research-Based Strategies

Recommended Texts
Putting the Pieces Together (elementary)
Books on secondary mental models

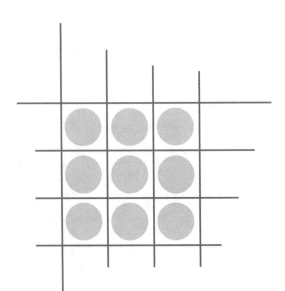

Process 1:
Data Analysis

Why Data Analysis?

- Allows you to determine how individual students are performing in relation to the overall population

- Helps predict your AYP (adequate yearly progress)/school rating

- Provides an approach to address federal mandates that require analysis of performance by student subgroups—and patterns of equity and excellence to be determined

- Allows you to quickly identify students needing intervention(s)

- Allows you to identify targeted populations for AYP goals

- Allows you to identify target standards

Many districts now have computer programs that can generate the grids; however, our experience has been that the usefulness of the information is diminished unless teachers themselves construct the grids. We have been told that the act of writing the student's name on the grid helps create a connection with the student and makes the information more meaningful to the teacher.

Benefits to Teachers

Provides a simple process to the teacher

- To understand individual student data

- To understand students that "count" in more than one category

- To understand areas of strengths and weakness so that instruction can be targeted

When instruction is targeted to specific needs of students with appropriate interventions, student achievement increases.

Student Data Grid

Grade Level:　　　　　　　　Content:

TEST BAND	Caucasian	African American	Hispanic	LSES *	LEP **	Disabled

* Low Socioeconomic Status
** Limited English Proficiency

This grid needs to be adapted based on the subgroups for a campus, as well as the performance categories of the state assessment. For example, the test band may include Advanced as the top band, followed by Proficient, followed by Basic, and then Below Basic. Some states have five performance categories, so the grid should be adapted accordingly.

Ideally, this grid would focus on percentiles for the test band because percentiles represent equal measures of growth. As such, it is easier to predict growth from band to band. However, the reality is that most states use scaled scores that are then translated into performance categories. Therefore, we encourage campuses to use the scaled scores and corresponding performance categories but to keep in mind that these scores may change from year to year, which has additional implications when working to raise student achievement.

A key is that teachers understand the categories, the "cut scores" for each category, and the subgroups for their campus. Also, do not exclude a subgroup of students even if they don't meet the required cohort number. These students will count in the district subgroup, which may have enough students across the district to be a required subgroup that counts toward AYP. Additionally, the scaled scores may vary by grade level and content area, so teachers must be given accurate information to complete the grids. Some states/districts also withhold the free and reduced-price lunch lists from teachers.

Tracking student progress by quartile helps measure student growth and determine the amount of probable progress in a given year. It helps us determine how many students, and specifically which students, we need to move.

Prediction guide: To achieve 80% passing on state assessment, 80% of students must score above 50% on a normed reference test.

Student Data Grid

Grade Level: Content:

TEST BAND	Caucasian	African American	Hispanic	LSES *	LEP **	Disabled
Advanced (500–725)	Joe 687 Scott 591 Laurie 586	Delicia 684 Lloyd 679	Juanita 693 Maria 589	Juanita 693	Juanita 693	Delicia 684
Proficient (400–499)	Jesse 465 Jeff 438 Megan 420 Candi 405	Dacoda 470 Jillian 434	Cecilia 471 Lu 410	Jesse 465 Jillian 434		Jesse 465 Megan 420
Basic (300–399)	Sandy 395 Casey 385			Sandy 395		Sandy 395
Below basic (below 300)		Jonas 295	Andrea 265	Jonas 295 Andrea 265	Andrea 265	Jonas 295 Andrea 265
Students who were exempt	Benjamin					Benjamin

* Low socioeconomic status
** Limited English proficiency

Steps:

1. Teachers complete this one-page grid for each class they teach. (See example above.) If a teacher has five sections of eighth-grade English, he/she will complete five separate grids. At the elementary level, teachers complete a grid for both math and reading.

2. Grids for science and writing also should be completed, even though the test is not given every year. If the campus is accountable for student performance in any other subject area, grids for that area also should be completed.

3. When completing the grid, teachers identify each student by ethnicity and level of performance. All students must be listed within an ethnic group.

4. If a student is included in other subgroups, he/she is listed again in the respective subgroup(s). This process enables teachers to see that some students "count" in multiple subgroups. The implication then is that raising the achievement of such students provides for a stronger payoff as they count in more than one subgroup.

The grid will allow teachers to check for patterns of achievement over time.

AYP/Predicting Rating
Grade Level/Department Results

TEST BAND 200	Caucasian 80	African American 80	Hispanic 40	LSES * 100	LEP ** 10	Disabled 40
Advanced	30	10	5	10	0	0
Proficient	30	30	15	30	2	20
Basic	15	20	10	20	3	10
Below basic	5	20	10	40	5	10
Students who were exempt						

* Low socioeconomic status
** Limited English proficiency

After teachers complete their individual grids, the principal compiles a grid for each content area and grade level to assess how the campus is progressing toward the current AYP target. For example, if the target is currently 80% of students proficient or above, that means 160 students (80% of 200 total students) must be scoring at a proficient level or higher. In this case only 120 students are proficient or advanced (determine this number by counting the number of students by ethnicity). The same process must be applied to each subgroup.

In this example, 64 Caucasian students must be proficient or advanced, and currently only 60 are. This is why teachers are asked to include student scores on the grid because the question now becomes: Of the 15 students in the basic category, which four could be expected to achieve proficiency in one year if there are specific, targeted interventions?

Apply this process to each subgroup to have a realistic understanding of students' performance against the goals. This process also can be applied to the teachers' individual class grids to determine how the group is performing against the AYP target (see page 12).

Utilizing such a process makes the data and the students more "real" for teachers and administrators alike. This process also allows school personnel to track student progress over time more easily since the information is on one page.

Questions to Consider

1. What patterns are evident from the data collection and grid process?

2. What are the areas of strength by content area/grade level?

3. What are the areas of concern by content area/grade level?

4. Which students have been identified as targets for specific remediation?

Key questions to ask about the results are listed above. You will note that this process also requires that teachers analyze weak and strong standards as well. For years, that was the focus of many schools; they looked at student performance by objective. And while that is important, focusing on individual students first is more important. It is not enough to focus solely on student performance by objective or student results by performance category; both are needed.

It is essential to keep in mind that "Accountability is based on *numbers* of students in a given category and the number or percentage of students who are moving to another category. It is not based on the group average" (Payne, 2008).

Applying AYP Activity to Individual Classroom

Teacher: _____

Grade: _____

Reading (Math) Social Studies Science Writing

Circle test data used

TEST BAND	ALL — Total # ___ X 80% = ___	CAUC — Total # ___ X 80% = ___	AA — Total # ___ X 80% = ___	HISP — Total # ___ X 80% = ___	Low SES — Total # ___ X 80% = ___	SPED — Total # ___ X 80% = ___	LEP — Total # ___ X 80% = ___
Advanced (2400–2600)	E. Smith 2484 E. Martinez 2484 K. Simmons 2484 C. Marshall 2477 B. Rodriguez 2400 B. Riley 2400	E. Smith 2484 C. Marshall 2477	K. Simmons 2484 B. Riley 2400	E. Martinez 2484 B. Rodriguez 2400	E. Martinez 2484 K. Simmons 2484 B. Rodriguez 2400 B. Riley 2400		E. Martinez 2484
Proficient (2100–2399)	T. Paine 2335 E. Tony 2280 J. Rivera 2255 M. Vargas 2231 L. Harris 2208 A. Inge 2186 K. Chapman 2142 W. James 2134	T. Paine 2335 E. Tony 2280 A. Inge 2186 W. James 2134	L. Harris 2208 K. Chapman 2142	J. Rivera 2255 M. Vargas 2231	T. Paine 2335 E. Tony 2280 J. Rivera 2255 M. Vargas 2231 L. Harris 2208 A. Inge 2186 K. Chapman 2142 W. James 2134	K. Chapman 2142 W. James 2134	E. Martinez 2484 M. Vargas 2231
Basic (1900–2099)	T. Wagner 2038 (3?) C. Kelley 2020 (4?) X. Jones 2020 (4?) R. Reves 2003 (5?) T. Hardy 1952 (8?)	T. Hardy 1952 (8?)	T. Wagner 2038 (3?) C. Kelley 2020 (4?) X. Jones 2020 (4?)	R. Reves 2003 (5?)	T. Wagner 2038 (3?) C. Kelley 2020 (4?) X. Jones 2020 (4?) R. Reves 2003 (5?) T. Hardy 1952 (8?)	T. Wagner 2038 (3?) C. Kelley 2020 (4?) X. Jones 2020 (4?) R. Reves 2003 (5?) T. Hardy 1952 (8?)	R. Reves 2003 (5?)
Below Basic (1899 or less)							
No Score	L. Brady L. Anderson		L. Brady L. Anderson		L. Brady L. Anderson	L. Brady	L. Anderson

Additional Discussion Questions

1. Which students missed the passing level by a slim margin?

2. Why is this student in this category?

3. Which students impact more than one subgroup?

4. Which students have been identified for specific remediation?

5. What specific interventions will be provided?

6. How can a resource analysis help identify interventions for targeted students?

7. Which students have not passed and need to pass to graduate from high school?

Gridding data is a mandatory first step when working with this school improvement model. It is not enough, however, to just grid the data. Rather the analysis and the professional dialog that occur when teachers collaborate over their data are what begins to happen to create needed change that will lead to improved student achievement.

The questions listed above can be used for this professional dialog, but this list is not exhaustive. What other questions might you add when analyzing the data?

As you begin to focus on interventions, keep in mind that a resource analysis is a first step when determining interventions, as it tends to be a waste of time to make an intervention that utilizes a resource that the student is missing. For more information about resources and resource analysis, see *A Framework for Understanding Poverty* (2005).

Facilitating the Process

Teacher materials needed:

1. State assessment data for previous and current students

2. Current student roster identifying students by:

   - Ethnicity

   - Socioeconomic status

   - Special populations, such as Special Education and Limited English Proficiency

To facilitate this process, campus administration should provide this information to the teachers. Teachers should not have to search out this information.

To expedite the gridding process, we encourage teachers to work in pairs. With a class roster before him/her, one teacher calls the student's name while the other finds the student's name and score on the master list. The student's ethnicity is identified so that the teacher can record the name and score in the appropriate space on the grid. While doing this, the partner is referencing other rosters to determine socioeconomic status and special population information.

Non-Tested Content Areas

If no data are available for the subject area:

- Grid the content most appropriate to the subject

- All teachers teach reading

At most grade levels, science is not tested and, in most states, social studies is not tested, so frequently no data are available for these content areas. Teachers in these content areas, however, are vitally important to overall student achievement and improvement. If the science standards most closely align with math skills, science teachers can grid those scores—but reading is included in all disciplines, so gridding the reading score is always appropriate.

While it is not necessary that elective teachers grid their students' data, it is important that they know which of their students have and have not passed state assessment. A simple "+" or "–" sign in the grade reporting document can provide this information.

Activity Options

Using a blank sheet of paper, set up the grid for your content area or grade level.

Or:

Using data from one class you currently teach, grid your students' scores. (Lists of students by ethnicity, free/reduced lunch, Special Education, and English Language Learners will be needed to complete the activity.)

Classroom Application

For optimal results, students should use:

- A consistent "plan and label" for math problem solving

- A consistent "plan and label" for nonfiction text

- A consistent strategy for open-response questions

Myriad factors contribute to a student struggling on state assessment. One factor could be the different ways that teachers from grade level to grade level teach core concepts and skills.

When teachers come to consensus on how these core skills, such as problem solving and nonfiction reading, are taught—and use the same strategy from grade level to grade level—learning can be accelerated because the students aren't having to take a different approach to learning each year. When mental models are used consistently to do this, they provide a "hook" for the students to retain the information. The same applies to a consistent strategy for open-response questions.

Plan and Label—QTIPS

Math Problem Solving

Letter	Step	Teacher Directions	Symbol	Sentence Starter
Q	Question	Use sentence frame to underline question		I was asked to ...
T	Think	Thoughtfully, thoroughly, and totally read problem		
I	Information	Circle important information and labels; cross out unnecessary information		I knew ...
P	Plan	Choose plan, operation, or strategy: OPERATION STRATEGY STEPS		I used ...
S	Solution	Show your work; choose your answer; check your answer	X = 10	The answer is ... because ...

Note. From Lodi Unified Schools, Morada Middle School, Stockton, CA, 2004–05.

QTIPS is a problem-solving model that provides a strategic approach to solving problems. When all students across the campus use the model, time is optimized as teachers are not spending time teaching different models. This also simplifies the process for lower performing students, as they have one model they use over and over; it does not change from year to year.

Reading Strategies

1. Box in and read the title.
2. Trace and number the paragraphs.
3. Stop and think at the end of each paragraph to identify a key point.
4. Circle the key word or write the key point in the margin.
5. Read and label the key words in the questions.
6. Prove your answer. Locate the paragraph where the answer is found.
7. Mark or write your answer.

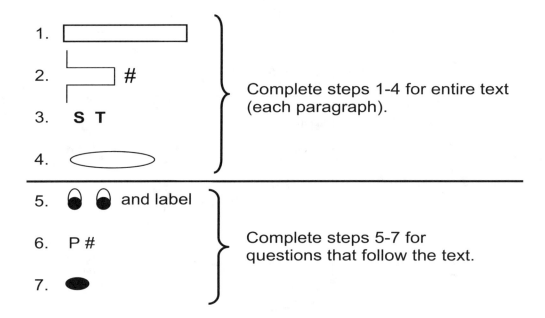

1.

2. #

3. **S T**

4.

Complete steps 1-4 for entire text (each paragraph).

5. and label

6. P #

7.

Complete steps 5-7 for questions that follow the text.

This "plan and label" exercise applies to nonfiction text. Most state assessments include a large amount of nonfiction text. When students are taught a process for approaching the text and practice this within the regular classroom, scores can increase. In addition to the English/reading teachers, this is a great model for science and social studies teachers, as well as non-core teachers whose curriculum includes reading.

U R TOPS

Strategy for Open-Response Questions

U	UNDERLINE	UNDERLINE or highlight key words, ideas, power verbs, and important information.
R	READ	READ everything twice before you start to answer. Read charts, diagrams, and maps, then reread the question.
T	TOPIC	Create a TOPIC SENTENCE that clearly states your position, decision, or starts your answer.
O	ORGANIZE	ORGANIZE your thoughts to answer the question. Be clear, concise, and to the point.
P	PART	Look for specific PARTS to be answered. Label each part with a number.
S	SUPPORT	SUPPORT your answer with facts, figures, or statements from what is given.

Note. From *Putting the Pieces Together*, by K. D. Ellis, 2004.

Some state assessments include open-response questions. Again, a learning strategy such as U R TOPS, which is a plan and label strategy, provides a strategic approach for students to utilize when answering these questions.

Data Analysis

Walk-Through Checklist

	Present	Needed	N/A
Teacher directly teaches planning behaviors for academic tasks			
Teacher requires student use of planning behaviors for academic tasks			
Teacher directly teaches a nonfiction reading strategy			
Teacher requires student use of a nonfiction reading strategy			
Teacher directly teaches a problem-solving model			
Teacher requires student use of a problem-solving model			

Four examples of checklists that can be used by administrators to monitor implementation of this process are included. These also provide a rubric for teachers to use to assess themselves regarding their implementation of these strategies.

For more information on how to utilize these checklists, see the Appendix that contains planning and monitoring tools to assist the principal.

Data Analysis

Walk-Through Checklist—QTIPS

	Present	Needed	N/A
QTIPS poster is displayed in classroom			
Work displayed in classroom shows QTIPS plan and label strategy			
Teacher references and models QTIPS in instruction			
Students use QTIPS in classwork as directed by teacher			
Students use QTIPS independently			
Students are writing about math using QTIPS sentence starters or CSRQ (complete sentence restates question)			
Grading/scoring is based on a process—QTIPS			

Data Analysis

Walk-Through Checklist—Reading Strategies

	Present	Needed	N/A
Reading Strategies poster is displayed in classroom			
Work displayed in classroom shows plan and label strategy			
Teacher references Reading Strategies in Instruction			
Teacher models Reading Strategies			
Students use Reading Strategies in classwork as directed by teacher			
Students use Reading Strategies independently			
Grading/scoring is based on a process—Reading Strategies			

Data Analysis

Walk-Through Checklist—U R TOPS

	Present	Needed	N/A
U R TOPS poster is displayed in classroom			
Work displayed in classroom shows U R TOPS planning strategy			
Teacher references and models U R TOPS in instruction			
Students use U R TOPS in classwork as directed by teacher			
Students use U R TOPS independently			
Students use U R TOPS strategy when writing their responses to open-response questions			
Grading/scoring is based on a process—U R TOPS			

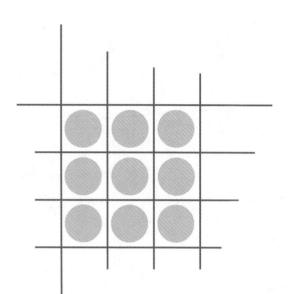

Process 2:
Assigning Time, Aligning Instruction

Why Assigning Time, Aligning Instruction?

- Identifies what the student has the opportunity to learn and the amount of time provided to learn it

- Addresses the focus of instruction by grading period

- Facilitates dialog about instruction, curriculum, and pedagogy

- Achieves consistency in instructional focus among teachers

Benefits to Teachers

- Provides a collegial and collaborative approach to determine reasonable expectations, specifically what will be taught each grading period and the amount of time that will be spent on it

- Is a simpler approach to curriculum mapping

- Involves all teachers in the process, which increases understanding of expectations and facilitates professional dialog related to instruction

- Provides a simpler way to understand what is taught by the preceding grade level so the teacher is better informed regarding skills that students should bring to the classroom

- Provides a simpler method to align the curriculum

- Provides a simpler model for teachers new to the grade-level/content area to understand the expectations regarding the instructional focus

- Allows the grade level to analyze student assessment results against what was actually taught and the time when it was taught; teachers can determine whether there was a payoff in the results from their efforts

Steps in Assigning Time, Aligning Instruction

Step 1: Each teacher develops his/her own grid by:

1. Dividing a sheet of paper into six or four equal sections, dependent on the grading period (six weeks or nine weeks in a grading period)

2. Listing the skills or units taught in each grading period, completing all grading periods for the year

3. Listing number of days of instruction to be spent per unit or skill

4. Listing total teaching days per grading period and comparing days from Step 3 to total for grading period (omit non-instructional days)

See examples of grids on the following pages.

What Is Being Taught?

First Nine Weeks	Second Nine Weeks
Third Nine Weeks	**Fourth Nine Weeks**

This is an example of a grid for a nine-week grading period.

What Is Being Taught?

First Six Weeks	Second Six Weeks	Third Six Weeks
Fourth Six Weeks	**Fifth Six Weeks**	**Sixth Six Weeks**

This is an example of a grid for a six-week grading period.

Step 2: All grade-level or department/course teachers meet

- Utilizing their grids from Step 1, state standards, and test scores …

    i. Teachers agree what will be taught
    ii. Teachers agree when it will be taught
    iii. Teachers agree on amount of time to teach it

- Teachers correlate state standards to units of instruction

In coming to consensus on what will be taught, when it will be taught, and the time to be spent teaching it, teachers are establishing the expectations for instruction for their own grade level. Key to this process is identifying state assessment dates and working backward to outline the units and skills for the year. Again, the standard(s), units, and time must all be included. Teachers must ensure that all standards are taught prior to the state test.

Sample Time and Content Grid

ELA Grade 11 Special Education   Second Quarter

Standard	Content	Time
F.12.1 E.12.4	Using the telephone: telephone books, telephone numbers, telephone service providers and bills, mobile phones, and phone cards.	6 classes 2 weeks
F.12.1	Using a library: what's in a library, fiction and nonfiction books, the Dewey Decimal System, periodicals and audiovisuals, and finding information in a library.	5 classes 1.5 weeks
A.12.1 A.12.2 A.12.3 B.12.1 E.12.4	Novel: *A Christmas Carol* Introduction: movie. Compare and contrast different versions. Read the novel: entertainment vs. social criticism.	10 classes 3.5 weeks
B.12.1 B.12.2 B.12.3	Business letters and forms: memos, applications, letters, reports, and résumés.	9 classes 3 weeks
	Semester exam	

Note. Developed by Dave Weyenberg, Menominee Indian High School, Keshena, WI.

This is an example of one-quarter of a nine-week grid that was compiled by a Special Education teacher. He included the number of classes and the correlation to time in his grid.

Step 3: Align instruction for content area or course

- Teachers meet by department or building (K–5, 6–8, or 9–12) to:

    i. Review course/grade-level documents
    ii. Ensure there are no gaps or repetition in what the student will have the opportunity to learn

- Subcommittee revises the documents, if necessary

- Revised documents are returned to the teachers for use in lesson planning and instruction

- Each year after state test results are analyzed, these documents are revised to reflect the instructional needs of the current group of students with whom the teachers will be working

The last step in this process provides a quick and simple way to align the curriculum. After teachers of a course or grade level come to consensus on their time and content grids, the alignment process (as noted above) begins.

While most districts and schools have curriculum guides, state curriculum documents, test blueprints, and numerous other curriculum resources, this process provides a teacher-friendly approach to curriculum development and alignment.

The principal uses these documents for grade-level/department meetings at least twice a year to check on progress in learning.

Analyzing Assessment Results Against Time and Content Grids

1. How does this time and content grid differ from what is actually taught?

2. What changes are needed based on the assessment results?

3. How is bellwork (see next page) used to reinforce the weak standards?

As in the gridding process, the dialog that occurs as teachers work through this process provides the opportunity for professional growth and understanding. This growth is furthered through discussion focusing on questions, such as those listed below.

Key questions to ask regarding changes based on assessment results include:

- When were the weakest standards taught?
- How much time was spent in direct instruction on the weakest standards?
- Did the students have time to learn the skill or concept?
- Was the standard taught during a period that had outside interference, such as immediately preceding a holiday?

What questions would you add to further your growth or the growth of your learning community?

Classroom Application

Bellwork (student independent work in first 5–7 minutes of class)

Bellwork provides an optimal means to reinforce weak standards. This work, written in the format of the state assessment, is completed at the beginning of the class period while the teacher takes attendance and attends to other administrative tasks. It should not take more than 5–7 minutes from class time. Reviewing the bellwork with the students and discussing response options is an opportunity for direct instruction and reinforcement of skills. It also provides insight into students' cognitive processing that can aid the teacher in assessing and addressing individual needs.

Example 1

The table below shows how many minutes Tim practiced playing the piano last weekend.

How many minutes did Tim practice the piano in all?

a. 72
b. 62
c. 92
d. 82

Day	Time (in minutes)
Friday	24
Saturday	30
Sunday	28

Create another question using the information on the grid on the back of your paper.

Example 2

Tim had a 10-dollar bill. He bought three hot dogs. Each hot dog cost $1.78 each, including tax.

A. How much change did Tim receive? _____

B. Use what you know about money/decimals to explain how you determined the amount of change Tim received. Use words and/or numbers in your explanation.

Example of Bellwork Schedule

Assessment Parameter	Date
Multiplying and dividing whole numbers	November 1
Using money/decimals in problem solving	November 8
Fractions: multiplying, dividing, and ordering	November 15
Interpreting and analyzing data in line graphs	November 29
Interpreting and analyzing data in bar graphs	December 5
Measurement	December 12

Based on the item analysis from the state assessment and 10-question tests (Process 4), teachers are encouraged to outline a schedule of bellwork for each grading period. Again, this is done collaboratively, and teachers can share the responsibility of developing the bellwork that will be used by the grade level/course so that no individual teacher is having to do all the work. This process also helps to close any gaps in instructional focus that may occur if students change teachers for some reason.

Activity

With colleagues, create a schedule of bellwork for the next grading period for one of your classes/courses.

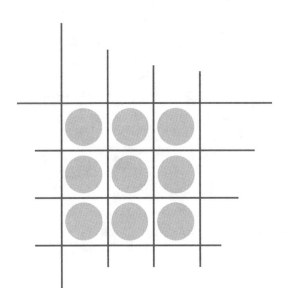

Process 3:

Assessment Context, State Assessment Glossary, Academic Vocabulary, Assessment Blueprint

Why Assessment Context, State Assessment Glossary, Academic Vocabulary, Assessment Blueprint?

- Establish context in which standards will be assessed

- Identify labels (vocabulary) needed for content and testing

- Create glossary of assessment terms

- Identify academic vocabulary

- Familiarize teachers with assessment blueprint

Most state education department websites provide a plethora of information about the state assessment. The extent to which this information is utilized may have a direct impact on teachers' understanding of the test and its level of expectations. Schools need a strategic means to analyze this information in order to provide a greater payoff in student achievement.

Benefits to Teachers

- Understanding the rules of a game increases the likelihood of success in the game

- Understanding the test blueprint, vocabulary, and assessment context is synonymous with understanding the rules of the game

Understanding Assessment Context

1. Find assessment context vocabulary or glossary

2. Look at assessment blueprint to identify percentages of questions from different areas

3. Identify context ("frames" in which standards will be assessed)

4. Identify performance categories

5. Identify standards

6. Pull key words from standards

7. Link key words from standards to appropriate context in blueprint

8. Analyze breakdown of questions against subskill or objective

Assessment context refers to the "frames" in which a standard will be assessed—i.e., in reading it could be a train schedule, a cookbook, an advertisement, technical writing, etc., and the skill level that will accompany that frame.

These steps outline the primary activities that help the teacher fully comprehend the expectations of the test.

Assessment Context

Glossary of Terms Used in Wisconsin Reading Assessment Framework

A

Affix. A word element added to the beginning (prefix) or the end (suffix) of a word to alter its meaning or part of speech, for example pre-, -ful, and -ly.

Alliteration. Repetition of an initial consonant sound across syllables or words (for example, "sleds sliding on snowy slopes").

Analogy. A comparison of two things that are similar in some way. Writers often use analogy to explain something unfamiliar by comparing it to something familiar.

Analyze. In Bloom's Taxonomy this refers to breaking down a text into its component parts in order to make the relationships between the ideas more explicit.

Anecdote. A short narrative that is often entertaining or used to illustrate a point and is presumed to be true.

Antonym. A word that means the opposite of another word.

Audience. The reader.

Note. From http://www.dpi.state.wi.us/

Not all states include a glossary of terms with their state blueprint. If they do, it is important that all teachers use the terms as they are defined in direct instruction. These glossaries can be shared with other departments for reinforcement as well. If your state does not provide a glossary of terms, teachers can develop their own from the state standards. Teachers are encouraged to make word walls as they teach the terms and to utilize the instructional strategy of sketching to determine if students understand the word. If they can sketch the word, they are much more likely to understand its meaning.

Test Blueprint Component

Wisconsin Blueprint for Reading Assessment

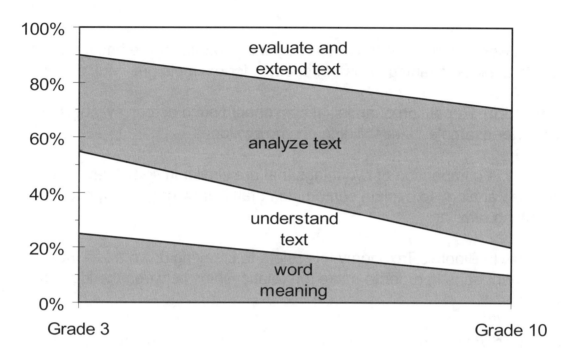

Note. From http://www.dpi.state.wi.us/

This blueprint provides a visual of the increasing demands of the test as a student progresses from Grade 3 to 10. For example, at Grade 3 approximately 25% of the test focuses on word meaning. By the time the student tests at Grade 10, word meaning comprises about 15% of the test. Understanding text is emphasized much less at Grade 10 than analyzing, evaluating, and extending text.

Test Blueprint Component

Wisconsin Blueprint for Reading Assessment

Table 6. Typical kinds of text at each grade level on the WKCE–CRT (Wisconsin Knowledge & Concepts Examination–Criterion-Referenced Test):

3–4
- Realistic fiction, animal stories, poetry, drama, folktales, fables, biography
- Nonfiction trade book excerpts, magazine articles
- Charts, schedules, menus, tickets, product labels, safety notices, school-related texts, simple instructions

5–6
- Realistic fiction, poetry, drama, biography, autobiography, historical fiction, myths
- Magazine, textbook, and newspaper articles; government documents
- Charts, schedules, simple forms, applications (for example, camp), product labels, safety notices, simple instructions

7–8
- Short stories, novel excerpts, poetry, drama, biography, autobiography
- Magazine, textbook, and newspaper articles; government documents, historical papers, reports, manuals, reviews, editorial cartoons
- Charts, schedules, forms, timelines, applications, product use or warning labels, safety notices, technical instructions

Note. From http://www.dpi.state.wi.us/

This portion of the blueprint identifies the kinds of text that are assessed by the state of Wisconsin by grade level.

Test Blueprint Component

Wisconsin Blueprint for Reading Assessment

General descriptions of proficiency categories:

Advanced: Demonstrates in-depth understanding of academic knowledge and skills tested on WKCE for that grade level.
Eighth-grade Reading: 539–790

Proficient: Demonstrates competency in the academic knowledge and skills tested on WKCE for that grade level.
Eighth-grade Reading: 480–538

Basic: Demonstrates some academic knowledge and skills tested on WKCE for that grade level.
Eighth-grade Reading: 445–479

Minimal performance: Demonstrates very limited academic knowledge and skills tested on WKCE for that grade level.
Eighth-grade Reading: 330–444

Note. From http://www.dpi.state.wi.us/

Another component of the test blueprint that is important for teachers to understand is the performance categories and the scaled scores associated with each category.

Wisconsin Blueprint for Reading Assessment

A. 4.1 Use effective reading strategies to achieve their purposes in reading	A. 8.1 Use effective reading strategies to achieve their purposes in reading	A. 12.1 Use effective reading strategies to achieve their purposes in reading
<ul><li>Use a variety of strategies and word recognition skills, including rereading, finding context clues, applying their knowledge of letter-sound relationships, and analyzing word structures</li><li>Infer the meaning of unfamiliar words in the context of a passage by examining known words, phrases, and structures</li><li>Demonstrate phonemic awareness by using letter/sound relationships as aids to pronouncing and understanding unfamiliar words and text</li><li>Comprehend reading by using such strategies as activating prior knowledge, establishing purpose, self-correcting and self-monitoring, rereading, making predictions, finding context clues, developing visual images, applying knowledge of text structures, and adjusting reading rate according to purpose and difficulty</li><li>Read aloud with age-appropriate fluency, accuracy, and expression</li><li>Discern how written texts and accompanying illustrations connect to convey meaning</li><li>Identify and use organizational features of texts—such as headings, paragraphs, and format—to improve understanding</li><li>Identify a purpose for reading, such as gaining information, learning about a viewpoint, and appreciating literature</li></ul>	<ul><li>Use knowledge of sentence and word structure, word origins, visual images, and context clues to understand unfamiliar words and clarify passages of text</li><li>Use knowledge of the visual features of texts, such as headings and bold face print, and structures of texts, such as chronology and cause and effect, as aids to comprehension</li><li>Establish purposeful reading and writing habits by using texts to find information, gain understanding of diverse viewpoints, make decisions, and enjoy the experience of reading</li><li>Select, summarize, paraphrase, analyze, and evaluate, orally and in writing, passages of texts chosen for specific purposes</li></ul>	<ul><li>Apply sophisticated word meaning and word analysis strategies—such as knowledge of roots, cognates, suffixes, and prefixes—to understand unfamiliar words</li><li>Gather information to help achieve understanding when the meaning of a text is unclear</li><li>Apply knowledge of expository structures, such as the deductive or inductive development of an argument, to the comprehension and evaluation of texts</li><li>Identify propaganda techniques and faulty reasoning in texts</li><li>Explain and evaluate the influence of format on the readability and meaning of a text</li><li>Distinguish between fact and opinion in nonfiction texts</li><li>Consider the context of a work when determining the meaning of abbreviations and acronyms, as well as the technical, idiomatic, and figurative meanings of terms</li></ul>

Note. From http://www.dpi.state.wi.us/

This grid identifies expectations of one reading standard for grades 4, 8, and 12.

Context for Assessment of Standards

A. 4.1 Use effective reading strategies to achieve their purposes in reading	A. 8.1 Use effective reading strategies to achieve their purposes in reading	A. 12.1 Use effective reading strategies to achieve their purposes in reading
<ul><li>Rereading</li><li>Context clues</li><li>Letter-sound relationships</li><li>Analyzing word structures</li><li>Phonemic awareness</li><li>Comprehend reading:<ul><li>activating prior knowledge</li><li>establishing purpose</li><li>self-correcting and self-monitoring</li><li>rereading</li><li>making predictions</li><li>context clues</li><li>developing visual images</li><li>text structures</li><li>adjust reading rate</li></ul></li><li>Organizational features:<ul><li>headings</li><li>paragraphs</li><li>format</li></ul></li><li>Identify purpose:<ul><li>gaining information</li><li>viewpoint</li><li>appreciating literature</li></ul></li></ul>	<ul><li>Word origins</li><li>Visual images</li><li>Context clues</li><li>Use visual features:<ul><li>headings</li><li>bold face print</li><li>structures of texts<ul><li>chronology</li><li>cause and effect</li></ul></li></ul></li><li>Understand diverse viewpoints</li><li>Make decisions</li><li>Enjoy the experience of reading</li><li>Select, summarize, paraphrase, analyze, and evaluate, orally and in writing, passages of texts chosen for specific purposes</li></ul>	<ul><li>Roots</li><li>Cognates</li><li>Suffixes</li><li>Prefixes</li><li>Expository structures:<ul><li>deductive</li><li>inductive development of an argument</li></ul></li><li>Propaganda techniques</li><li>Faulty reasoning</li><li>Fact and opinion in nonfiction texts</li><li>Consider the context of a work when determining the meaning of abbreviations and acronyms as well as the technical, idiomatic, and figurative meanings of terms</li></ul>

Note. Adapted from materials found at http://www.dpi.state.wi.us/

This grid breaks down the standard into the core skills needed for success on the assessment; it provides a simpler way to understand the level of expectation of the standard, as well as the context in which the standard will be assessed.

Classroom Application

- Word walls

- Vocabulary sketching

Word walls are simply "words on the wall" that are associated with units of instruction. Words are added as they are taught, so the wall often changes. However, some key academic terms may remain throughout the year. Numerous word wall samples are available online if some ideas are needed to get started.

As administrators conduct walk-throughs, they should look for evidence of word walls that align to current units of instruction. Examples of vocabulary sketching also can be posted in the room or on the word wall to indicate implementation of the strategy. Talking to students about how frequently they sketch vocabulary or asking students to show an example of their vocabulary work is another excellent means of monitoring.

Examples of Sketching

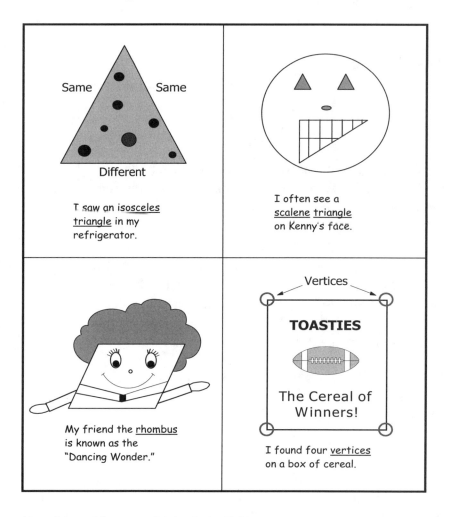

Note. Adapted from materials by Cathy Fields.

When students can sketch a vocabulary word, they tend to have a much better understanding of its meaning. If they cannot, it usually indicates they have little or no understanding of the word. This is a simple and quick means to assess their understanding. Because the sketching also is a mental model, it is more likely they will retain the meaning of the word. These are student examples of sketching activities using certain math terms: isosceles triangle, scalene triangle, rhombus, and vertices.

Activity

Identify academic vocabulary associated with state assessment or with an upcoming unit that you would include on a word wall for your classroom.

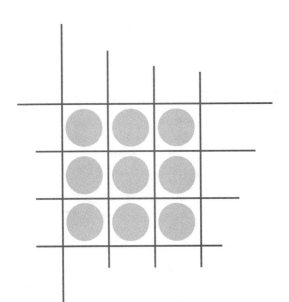

Process 4:
Ten-Question Tests—
First Semester

Why 10-Question Tests?

- Grades are not always a measure of what was learned; instead they often measure effort and compliance, so a more accurate form of measurement is needed

- A system (test) is needed that assesses standards taught each quarter/grading period so you can quickly identify students who are not mastering the standards taught during the grading period

- These tests enable you to analyze individual student and group progress against the standards each quarter/grading period

- They also allow you to design and implement interventions immediately for students who are struggling

Benefits to Teachers

By utilizing 10-question tests to identify students not mastering the standards, teachers:

- Can intervene more quickly and address the learning needs of each student

- Make immediate interventions, which increases the likelihood of student success on state assessments

- Can ensure relationship between what is taught and what is assessed each grading period because these are teacher-generated

What Is a 10-Question Test?

- Questions that are added to a six-week or nine-week test to "dipstick" for students' progress against the standards (Payne, 2008)

- Teachers write or select the questions they will include on the test

- Teachers agree to use the same questions on the test

Two important elements about 10-question tests are:
- Questions are written in the format of state assessment questions
- Ten is not a magical number; the key is to include enough questions to adequately assess the standards but keep the test simple enough to easily grade and monitor

Steps to Create

1. Bring together test questions already used

2. Code questions with the standard numbers/indicators

3. Use the time and content grid to identify standards taught each grading period

4. Sort/eliminate questions by standard; find questions that best assess that standard

5. Embed questions into each teacher's test for the grading period (Payne, 2008)

Because teachers of the grade level/course are using the same 10-question tests, the easiest way to work through this process is for each teacher to select several questions he/she wants to include. Then, as a group, the "10" are selected for inclusion on the test. Once again, the professional dialog associated with the process and decision making for the questions will benefit the group.

Administration Responsibilities

With leadership team:

- Identify the testing dates

- List testing expectations, such as (1) do not review for the test or preview the test questions, (2) use testing tools (highlighters, calculators, reference sheets), and (3) use plan and label processes

Ideally, dates for administering and analyzing 10-question tests are established at the beginning of the year. These are included on a calendar so that everyone is aware of the testing times and can plan accordingly. Additional steps in planning for and implementing this process are available in the Appendix (see Administrator Checklist: Ten-Question Test).

Analysis of 10-Question Tests

1. Grade 10-question tests

2. Identify students by score on the data grid

3. Conduct an item analysis of the test data

4. Identify by student and class the weakest items by standard

5. Create a plan to remediate weak standards for each group/class

6. Identify individual student interventions

7. Identify current AYP goal

8. For each class, assess progress toward AYP goal

The analysis of the 10-question test is a critical step in this entire process of school improvement. Too often assessments are given, but time is not taken to review and utilize the results to address students' needs. Some teachers choose to have the students grade these particular questions on the test so that they can see their mistakes. Discussing the response choices also provides the teacher the opportunity to explain why the test maker selected those responses—e.g., the distinguishing characteristic between/among the choices, how the test writer was trying to "trick" the test taker, the patterns that become evident in the choices, etc.

These tests are not used to give another grade to the students, but instead they identify students who are struggling in relation to the standards taught that grading period.

Example of Questions from Third-Grade 10-Question Test

GRADE 3: SECOND SIX WEEKS

1. There are 273 students in second grade, 320 in third grade, and 297 in fourth grade. How many students are in the three grades combined?

   A. 880 students

   B. 780 students

   C. 890 students

   D. 990 students

2. The graph represents the number of pieces of fruit in the basket.

   Which chart matches the graph?

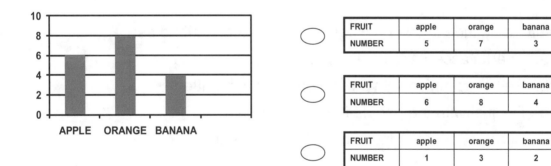

FRUIT	apple	orange	banana
NUMBER	5	7	3

FRUIT	apple	orange	banana
NUMBER	6	8	4

FRUIT	apple	orange	banana
NUMBER	1	3	2

This is one example of questions on a 10-question test. Note the difference in the format of the questions, as they should be written in the format of the state assessment.

Example of Questions from Secondary Language Arts' 10-Question Test

6. What type of poetic device is the author using in the phrase "The days of the far off future would toil onward"?

   a. Metaphor

   b. Allusion

   c. Personification

   d. Alliteration

7. The author, Nathaniel Hawthorne, uses the following narrative pattern in the passage:

   a. Persuasive

   b. Descriptive

   c. Cause and effect

   d. Compare and contrast

8. Hester's attitude in this passage can be best described as:

   a. Fearful acceptance of the punishment given to her

   b. Self-satisfaction with the actions she committed

   c. Disgust with the people in her community

   d. Scorn at the harshness of her punishment

9. The tone of the passage can best be described as:

   a. Suspenseful

   b. Happy

   c. Contented

   d. Spiteful

Note. Developed by Jennifer Meka Ratka.

While each of these questions is a multiple-choice question, note the level of questions that are being assessed.

Ten-Question Test: Item Analysis

Student Name	5.1	5.3	5.4	5.5	5.6	5.8a	5.9	5.10b	5.11	5.13a	Totals
Sam	-	-	+	-	+	+	-	-	-	-	-7
Pete	+	+	+	+	+	+	+	+	+	+	-0
Juan	-	-	+	-	+	+	-	-	-	+	-6
Natasha	+	+	+	+	+	+	+	+	-	+	-1
Kelly	+	+	+	+	+	+	-	-	-	+	-3
Erin	+	+	+	+	+	+	+	-	-	+	-2
Anthony	-	-	+	+	+	+	+	+	-	+	-3
Elena	+	+	+	+	+	+	+	+	+	+	-0
Denise	-	-	+	+	+	+	+	-	-	+	-4
Renee	+	+	+	+	+	+	+	+	+	+	-0
Thomas	-	-	+	+	+	+	+	+	-	-	-4
Nathan	+	+	+	+	-	+	+	+	+	-	-2
Jared	-	+	+	+	+	+	+	-	-	-	-4
Bobby	-	-	+	-	+	+	-	-	-	-	-7
Totals by Standard	7	6	0	3	1	0	4	7	10	5	

This tally sheet, identifying students who need intervention and standards that need to be retaught, is a simple means to make the assessment meaningful and useful. According to Guskey (2003), "The best classroom assessments also serve as meaningful sources of information for teachers, helping them identify what they taught well and what they need to work on. Gathering this vital information does not require a sophisticated statistical analysis of assessment results. Teachers need only make a simple tally of how many students missed each assessment item or failed to meet a specific criterion."

Question Analysis Form

QUESTION	YES	NO	COMMENT
1. Does the question go with the standard?			
2. Is there a correct answer?			
3. Is there more than one correct answer?			
4. Does the answer go with the question?			
5. Does the question discriminate by race, gender, age, or economic class?			
6. Are the wrong-answer choices (distracters) appropriate for the question?			
7. Does the stem mirror the state assessment?			
8. Is the question too specific to a particular kind or aspect of information?			
9. Does the question assess in the same manner the students are taught?			
10. Is the readability appropriate for the grade level assessed?			
11. Is the difficulty of the passage (vocabulary, concept, sentence, complexity, topic) appropriate to the grade level?			
12. Is the vocabulary/terminology used in instruction?			
13. Is the stem (question part of the question) clearly phrased?			
14. Is this question part of any unit that is taught?			
15. Does this question require prior knowledge?			
16. What is the P value of the question?			
17. Is the question formatted appropriately?			
18. Are the directions clear?			

Note. From *Learning Structures* (p. 77), by R. K. Payne, 2005.

As teachers work with 10-question tests and focus on continuous improvement, this form can be used to analyze the quality of the questions. As you work through the questions, it also is important to make sure that the questions address the level and expectations of the standards.

Mental Model for Part to Whole

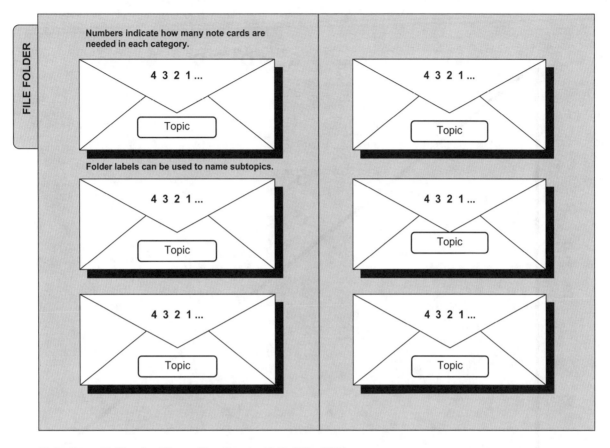

Note. From *Putting the Pieces Together,* by K. D. Ellis, 2004.

A mental model is a story, metaphor, analogy, or two-dimensional drawing that helps one translate from the concrete to the abstract. It tells either the structure, purpose, or pattern of the discipline or subject area (Payne, 2002).

Mental models are used to teach the key concepts of the discipline. When analyzing 10-question tests, it is important to identify the mental models that were used to teach the concepts/ standards that were assessed. If most students missed a question, was a mental model even taught with it? If so, what might students have failed to understand about the mental model that led to their missing the question? When used with consistency, mental models can help close the gaps in learning that are created when students have not been mediated from an early age. This consistency also can help students retain the concepts because different teachers are not teaching the same concept in different ways.

This mental model provides a sorting mechanism for a research project.

Mental Model of Pythagorean Theorem

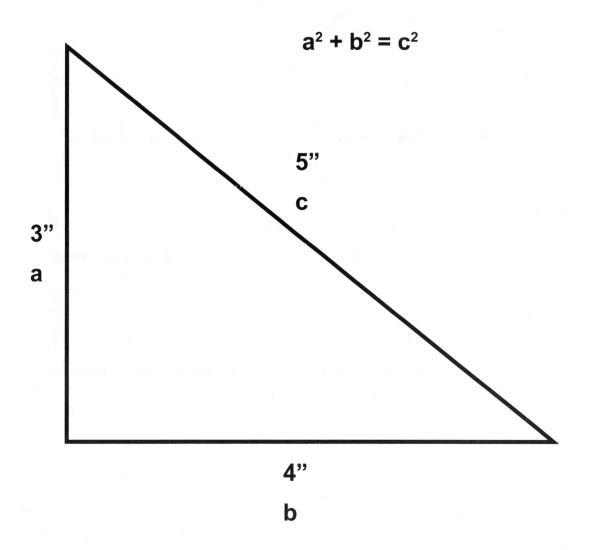

$$a^2 + b^2 = c^2$$

Note. From *Research-Based Strategies* (pp. 59–60), by R. K. Payne, 2009.

Mental Model of Pythagorean Theorem

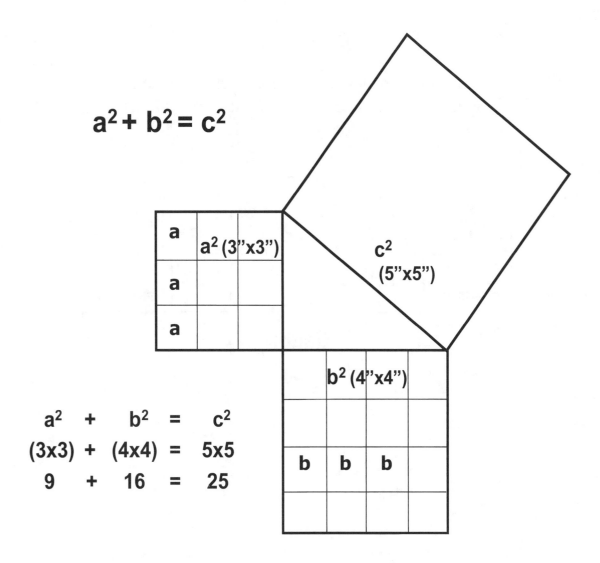

This illustration provides the mental model proving that $a^2 + b^2 = c^2$.

Mental Model for Liquid Measurement

Gallon Guy

1 Gallon	= 4 Quarts		1 Gallon	=	4 Quarts
1 Quart	= 2 Pints		1 Gallon	=	8 Pints
1 Pint	= 2 Cups		1 Gallon	=	16 Cups

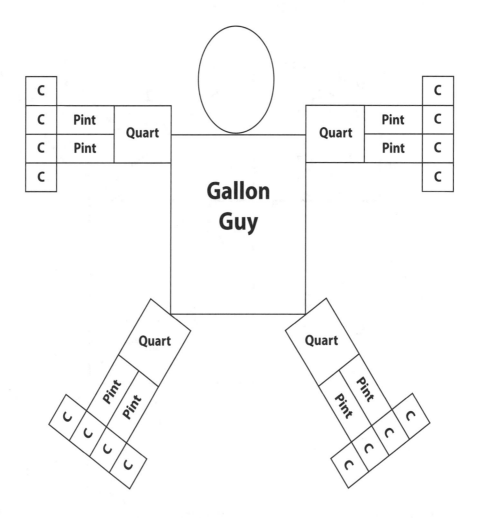

Note. From *Putting the Pieces Together,* by K. D. Ellis, 2004.

Liquid measurement is challenging for many students. When you teach them the Gallon Guy mental model, they remember 4 cups equal 2 pints or 1 quart; they remember 4 quarts equal one gallon—or 16 cups equal one gallon.

Classroom Application

Utilize specific mental models to help students learn faster and hold the information longer.

Activity

Identify or create one mental model that you will use in teaching a current unit or lesson.

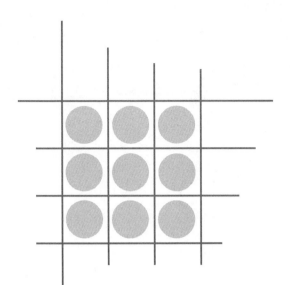

Process 5:
Interventions,
Data Analysis,
Grade Distribution,
Failure Rate

Why Interventions, Data Analysis, Grade Distribution, Failure Rate?

- Determine what to do when students do not learn the content

- Target interventions against data results

- Analyze grade distribution and failure rate to identify students for intervention and to correlate to other measures of achievement

Benefits to Teachers

- Timely interventions that are targeted to specific needs of students increase the likelihood of student success

- Success begets success for both the student and the teacher

- Relationships of mutual respect can be developed when teachers maintain high expectations but provide support through successful interventions for students

- Reflection on teacher practice can improve one's skills and knowledge

To Begin Sorting Causes of Inadequate Growth, These Questions Are Asked:

1. Is there a relationship issue? Does the student have a group to belong to?

2. Is there an issue with the paper world—the abstract representational world?

3. Is it a resource issue?

4. Is there a skills issue?

5. Is there a biochemical issue?

6. Is there a curriculum issue? (Was it actually taught?)

7. Did the student have enough time to learn it?

8. Was the work assigned on grade level (curriculum calibration)? (Payne, 2008)

Interventions for some students must be made at both the classroom and campus level. As much as possible, students should be kept in the regular classroom to receive "on-grade-level instruction"; they need the opportunity to learn what their peers are learning. Therefore, time must be created in the schedule for additional interventions—outside the regular classroom.

To better understand people from poverty,
the definition of poverty will be:

"The extent to which an individual
does without resources."

–Ruby K. Payne

Resources

Financial
Having the money to purchase goods and services

Language
Being able to speak and use formal register in writing and in speech

Emotional
Being able to choose and control emotional responses, particularly to negative situations, without engaging in self-destructive behavior; this is an internal resource and shows itself through stamina, perseverance, and choices

Mental
Having the mental abilities and acquired skills (reading, writing, and computing) to deal with daily life

Spiritual
Believing in divine purpose and guidance

Physical
Having physical health and mobility

Support Systems
Having friends, family, and backup resources available to access in times of need; these are external resources

Relationships/Role Models
Having frequent access to adult(s) who are appropriate, who are nurturing to the child, and who do not engage in self-destructive behavior

Knowledge of Hidden Rules
Knowing the unspoken cues and habits of a group

Note. From *A Framework for Understanding Poverty,* by R. K. Payne, 2005.

Resources provide the starting place for making interventions. When doing this, begin with the strongest resource and identify an intervention that will work that utilizes that resource. For example, if a student is not doing homework and has parental support, he/she has a support system that can be accessed to address the issue of homework. Keep in mind that relationships are a key motivator for students from poverty, so establishing a relationship of mutual respect between a staff member and student can have an impact on student success as well.

Activity

RESOURCE TO BE DEVELOPED	HOW IT AFFECTS SCHOOL PERFORMANCE	POSSIBLE INTERVENTIONS

- This is an excellent activity for a faculty meeting. Divide the nine resources among the faculty.
- On chart paper, invite each group to identify ways the resource affects school performance—
- and interventions that are already in place or could be provided to develop the resource. The School Improvement Team can then use these lists as they work with students and parents on intervention plans.

Resource Analysis

Name	Financial resources	Emotional resources	Mental resources	Spiritual resources	Physical resources	Support systems	Relationships/role models	Knowledge of hidden rules	Language

Completing this resource checklist for students who are struggling provides a quick reference for teachers when analyzing behaviors of students. Remember, the checklist does not have to be completed for every student but only for those who are struggling.

Resources: in Summary

Why look at resources?

Resources tell you where to make interventions.

Where do you start with interventions?

Start by working from strengths.

Why do you look at relationships first?

Relationships provide motivation for learning.

Dr. James Comer, an educator at Yale University, says this: "No significant learning occurs without a significant relationship [of mutual respect]."

Learning requires human interaction. At the heart of virtually all learning is relationship.

Note. All material on this page adapted from *Under-Resourced Learners* (pp. 14, 24), R. K. Payne, 2008.

Grade Distribution

Complete a grade distribution for the first semester.

Teacher	Total students in class	# A's	# B's	# C's	# D's	# F's
Class/period						

This grid can be used for tracking the distribution of grades for each class. Two questions to consider when analyzing the results are: (1) Is there alignment in the grades and actual performance of the students? And (2) if you teach multiple sections of the same course, is there a significant difference in the grades? If so, why?

Classroom Application

- Identify students who are struggling—based on 10-question test performance, state assessment, grades, or other campus measures

- Conduct a resource analysis of the student

- Teachers complete the On Ramp/Off Ramp activity at a staff meeting to identify interventions already in place and those still needed

Directions for On Ramp/Off Ramp activity:

1. Divide the staff into groups of four or five. Each group is given a piece of chart paper divided in half and labeled "Off Ramps" and "On Ramps."
2. Thinking of education as a freeway, each group brainstorms "off ramps" (actions/ behaviors that take them off course) that some students take during their school years.
3. Responses are listed on the chart.
4. Each group also brainstorms "on ramps" (those interventions and supports that help students stay on course or get back on course and refocused).
5. Responses are listed on the chart.

The administrator then asks the group to identify which of the interventions are "wait to fail" models. In other words, which are available to students only after they have already failed? The real issue becomes what can be done to prevent students from taking the "off ramp" in the first place and thereby help prevent their failure.

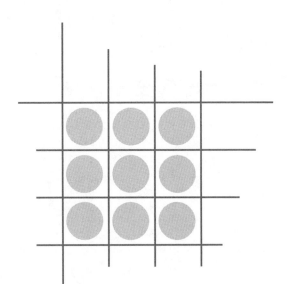

Process 6:

Content Comprehension—Processes, Step Sheets, Planning, RTI, Mental Models

Why Content Comprehension—Processes, Step Sheets, Planning, RTI, Mental Models?

- Content comprehension identifies what is more important and what is less important to a discipline/content area

- Teachers must understand the content comprehension of their discipline in order to get high achievement from students

Benefits to Teachers

- Understanding content comprehension (the purpose, patterns, structures, and processes) of one's content allows teachers to spend time on the instructional strategies and concepts that students really need to know and understand

- This knowledge, along with the use of mental models, can close the gap in understanding and achieving that under-resourced students often need; using mental models compresses instruction and gives students a way to hold information in their head (because of this, mental models help students master the multi-process assessment items that comprise a large percentage of state assessments)

- Step sheets and planning provide strategic approaches to tasks and texts that enable students to be more successful

- RTI enables the teacher to select appropriate interventions and monitor student progress against those interventions

Content Comprehension

- Process—the "how" of the content, e.g., math: multiplication, subtraction, addition, or division

- Purpose—why the content is studied

- Structures—basic forms of the content, literally the forms that are central to the understanding, e.g., math: numbers, space, time

- Patterns—units of study, the vocabulary in context

All content has processes, purpose, structures, and patterns. These determine what is more important and less important to the content area. Good teachers have content comprehension of their discipline, meaning they understand the content at such a deep level they can manipulate and use it. Knowing the purpose, structure, patterns, and processes, along with the vocabulary of the content area, are necessary when manipulating the content. It is these factors that tell you what is most important as you sort information in order to use it. Understanding these factors is also important in getting high achievement with students (Payne, 2009). To see examples, please refer to Strategy 2 in *Research-Based Strategies.*

Plan, Do, Review

PLAN FOR THE DAY	STEPS TO DO	REVIEW (HOW DID I DO?)
Task	1.	
	2.	
	3.	
	4.	
		Rubric
Task	1.	
	2.	
	3.	
		Checklist
Task	1.	
	2.	
		Assessment

The following pages contain examples of step sheets for planning, which also help establish procedural self-talk, mental models, and vocabulary sketching activities. All are helpful in developing content comprehension in students.

Five Generic Mental Models for Dealing with School and Work

Space	Provides organization Helps with math and maps
Formal register	Uses the language of money Has shared understanding
Part to whole	Allows for task completion
Time	Controls impulsivity Is about planning
Decoding	Can read the language and abstract symbols

Note. From *Learning Structures* (p. 9), by R. K. Payne, 2005.

Sketching Vocabulary Activity

Name: _____

Word	Picture
Love	
Religion	
Divorce	
Détente	
Egregious	

Give the first word and have the participant sketch it, then the second word, etc. Include a couple of words that might be less familiar to most persons to make the point that if one has a mental image or picture, there is probably a good understanding of the word's meaning. Without the picture, there is much less likelihood of understanding.

Sketching Vocabulary Activity

Name: _____

Word	Picture
Love	
Smile	
Cloud	
Star	
Dog	

Mental Models Help Students Translate from Abstract to Concrete

Mental Model for Kinds of Sentences

Declarative—A declarative sentence **makes a statement** and ends with a period.

Example: The dog found his bone.

Interrogative—An interrogative sentence asks a question and ends with a question mark.

Example: How many students are in this room?

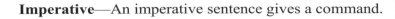

Imperative—An imperative sentence gives a command.

Example: Sit still and listen.

Exclamatory—An exclamatory sentence **shows strong feeling** and ends with an exclamation mark.

Example: This movie is scary!

Note. From *Mental Models for English/Language Arts: Grades 1–6.*

Mental Models Help Students Translate from Abstract to Concrete

Place Value

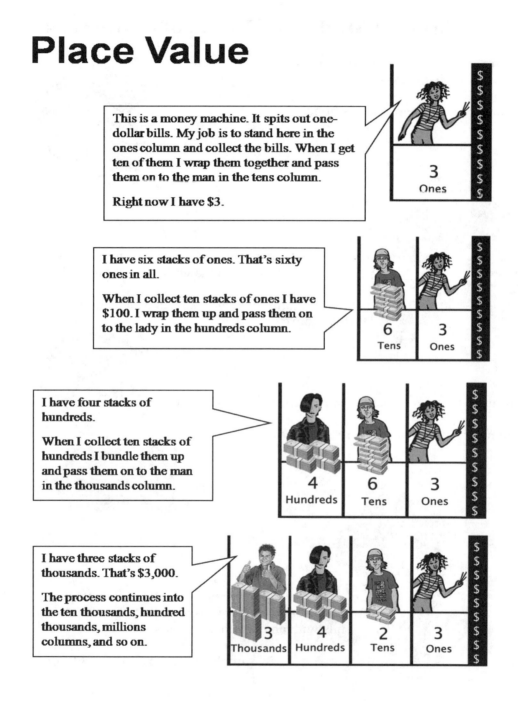

This is a money machine. It spits out one-dollar bills. My job is to stand here in the ones column and collect the bills. When I get ten of them I wrap them together and pass them on to the man in the tens column.

Right now I have $3.

I have six stacks of ones. That's sixty ones in all.

When I collect ten stacks of ones I have $100. I wrap them up and pass them on to the lady in the hundreds column.

I have four stacks of hundreds.

When I collect ten stacks of hundreds I bundle them up and pass them on to the man in the thousands column.

I have three stacks of thousands. That's $3,000.

The process continues into the ten thousands, hundred thousands, millions columns, and so on.

Note. From *Mental Models for Math: Grades 6–12.*

Classroom Application

- Research-based strategies

- Targeted interventions

Response to Intervention (RTI) requires that schools provide interventions for students who are not achieving success in the classroom. While there are specific mandates and requirements associated with RTI, a key is that interventions be targeted to specific needs. Ruby Payne's Research-Based Strategies is organized in such a way that specific interventions are recommended for observed behavioral and academic needs. For more information about RTI, also see Strategy 51 in Research-Based Strategies.

Student Intervention Plan Sheet

Student_____

RDG   MATH   OTHER
SES   SPED   LEP

	STANDARDS BEING ADDRESSED						
Proficiency Goal							
Performance Level							
Interventions		Date Started		Date Ended			
Responsible Party							
Evaluation							

Note. Developed by Shelley Rex.

This form provides a tool for developing an intervention plan. As with any intervention, the plan must be monitored and adjustments made if the intervention is not effective.

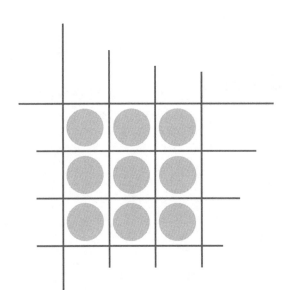

Process 7:
Ten-Question Tests—
Second Semester

Why 10-Question Tests?

- Grades are not always a measure of what was learned; instead they often measure effort and compliance, so a more accurate form of measurement is needed

- A system (test) is needed that assesses standards taught each quarter/grading period so you can quickly identify students who are not mastering the standards taught during the grading period

- These tests enable you to analyze individual student and group progress against the standards each quarter/grading period

- They also allow you to design and implement interventions immediately for students who are struggling

Benefits to Teachers

- For 10-question tests, benefits are the same as noted in Process 4

- Having students write their own questions increases students' cognitive skills and understanding

- Increasing students' cognition advances their knowledge to a higher level

Ten-Question Tests

Steps and processes included in Process 4 are repeated for this process, but the focus is on development of the tests for the second semester.

Classroom Application: Writing Multiple-Choice Questions

Question:
a.
b.
c.
d.

Three rules:
1. One wrong-answer choice must be funny.
2. Only one answer choice can be right.
3. May not use "all of the above," "none of the above," etc.

Teaching students to ask questions is an important cognitive skill. Some students cannot ask questions syntactically and, without this ability, the mind cannot know what it knows. Instead of asking the question syntactically, the student might ask it as a statement but through tone of voice—e.g., "You won't let me leave?" rather than "Won't you let me leave?" Doing any task requires that students be able to ask questions inside their head. If they cannot, they are unable to examine their own behavior, and they cannot retrieve information in a systematic way.

In this example of question making, students write their own question/answer choices, using the rules for their choices. Teachers then debrief with students about how the questions are written and may even give extra credit if a student's question is used on an exam. It is recommended that students work in pairs when completing this task. Additionally, having students develop their own questions twice a week will develop cognitive capacity and raise test scores.

TIP: At the second-grade level, limit answer choices to two—one right and one wrong (Payne, 2009).

Activity

In pairs, write a multiple-choice question, using the guidelines previously outlined, on a topic provided by the presenter.

Questions will be debriefed with the larger group.

Classroom Application

- Students develop multiple-choice questions at least twice a week
- Students analyze questions to understand content and verbiage

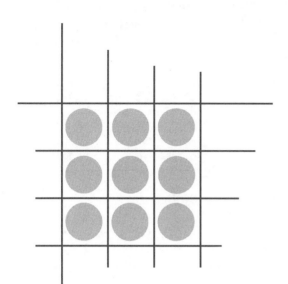

Process 8:
Curriculum Calibration, Artifacts Analysis, Rubrics

Why Curriculum Calibration, Artifacts Analysis, Rubrics?

- Ensure that the level of assignments matches the expectations of the state standards

- Utilize a variety of evidence in determining mastery of a concept

- Improve consistency of expectations among grade levels/departments

Benefits to Teachers

- Analyzing student work samples through professional dialog with colleagues helps the teacher ensure that expectations are aligned with the standards

- This dialog with colleagues promotes the sharing of best practices

- Use of the state writing rubric across disciplines (indeed, any rubric for projects) enables the teacher to identify expectations for students (and parents) from the beginning

- Use of a rubric promotes more objective grading

What Was Quality of Teaching?

High-quality teaching includes:

- Classroom management

- Instruction

- Content understanding and knowledge

High-quality teaching also involves the nature of the assignments. The types of assignments given to students and the level of expectations regarding the assignments are two indicators of quality.

Numerous studies document the importance of the teacher on student learning. The components in this process are designed to engage teachers in professional dialog that can help improve their practice. It begins with a description of high-quality teaching, which includes the nature of assignments that are given. The dialog then focuses on the calibration of the assignment to the standards and an analysis of the assignment itself.

	Mathematics GLS* Percentage * generalized least squares						Avg. Grade Level	Language Arts GLS Percentage						Avg. Grade Level
Grade	K	1	2	3	4	5		K	1	2	3	4	5	
K	100						K	100						K
1st		100					1.0		100					1.0
2nd		23	77				1.8		20	80				1.8
3rd			45	55			2.6		2	14	84			2.8
4th			40	40	20		2.8		2	30	35	33		3.0
5th		2	35	59	2	2	2.7			28	60	10	2	2.9

Note. From research study, by John Hollingsworth and Silvia Ybarra titled "Analyzing Classroom Instruction: Curriculum Calibration": http://www.dataworks-ed.com/ (chart found at: http://pubs.cde.ca.gov/tcsii/ documentlibrary/curiclumcalbration.asp)

This grid reflects research done by John Hollingsworth and Sylvia Ybarra and was included in a paper titled "Analyzing Classroom Instruction: Curriculum Calibration" from Dataworks Educational Research (http://www.dataworks-ed.com/). Note the number of assignments that are on grade level in kindergarten and first grade versus those on grade level at fifth grade. The question becomes, "How does this happen?" As Dr. Ybarra stated, "Student learning will never go higher than assignments we give them" (conversation between author Magee and Dr. Ybarra on May 20, 2003).

Rubric Guidelines

1. The purpose is to identify desired level of achievement and to set standard

2. The rubric must be simple and easy to understand; if a student is to use it, he/she must be able to understand it

3. Student growth toward the desired level of achievement must be clear; the extent to which the student has met the standard also must be clear

4. The rubric can be changed to meet the need

Note. From Meeting Standards & Raising Test Scores PowerPoint, by R. K. Payne and D. S. Magee, 2005.

Evaluation is at the highest level of Bloom's Taxonomy (1956). Evaluation requires criteria. And you need to know what criteria identify a skilled thinker in your content area. It is these criteria that sort what is important from what is less important. While, from the outset, rubrics are helpful for teachers and students to understand levels of expectations and mastery, they are probably most useful when used by students to self-assess their work.

There are numerous websites that provide rubrics for content areas; in addition, most states have rubrics for writing, and some also have them for math. These state rubrics are most effective when they are used by all staff, including those in cross-curricular areas. Rubrics can be adapted to be grade level appropriate as well. Finally, the rubrics provide a more accurate representation of a student's work than a numerical or letter grade.

When writing your own rubrics, the following guidelines can be useful.

Developing a Rubric

1. Identify 3–5 criteria

2. Set up a grid with numerical values; 1–4 is usually enough

3. Identify what would be an excellent piece of work; that becomes a 4

4. Work backward; identify what would be a 3, a 2, and so on; what would be unacceptable? that becomes a 1

Note. From Meeting Standards & Raising Test Scores PowerPoint, by R. K. Payne and D. S. Magee, 2005.

When developing a rubric oneself, these are guidelines that can be followed. Numerous rubrics are available online as well if one chooses to review them and look for appropriate models.

Benefits of Rubrics

1. Identify for students what they must do to make a desired grade

2. Provide opportunity for teachers to carefully consider what students are expected to learn, as well as what they are teaching

3. For all stakeholders—teachers, parents, students—expectations for performance are made clear

4. Feedback, reflection, and continuous learning can result when using rubrics

Note. From "Rubrics in Education: Old Term, New Meanings" (pp. 54–55), by S. Cooper and A. Gargan, *Kappan,* September 2009.

The benefits of rubrics appear to be clear. Working with rubrics, however, does require extra time initially. One recommendation is that when beginning to assess using rubrics, teachers score papers, then meet collaboratively to score the papers of their colleagues. A question to ask: Is there consistency in our scores? If not, what is creating the difference(s)?

Reading Rubric, Grade 5

Student Name: _____ School Year: _____

Campus: _____ Grade: _____

	Beginning	Developing	Capable	Expert
Fluent	Rate of reading interferes with meaning	Occasionally rate of reading interferes with meaning	Analyzes selection and uses most effective reading	Can articulate demands of reading task
Constructive	Has trouble understanding meaning of text Vocabulary slows reader	Can understand text but has difficulty formulating questions Can use text to make meaning of new vocabulary	Can explain why text is important and can summarize main points Can ask questions about text	Assigns meaning and relates information in larger context of knowledge Applies vocabulary outside of text and uses it to refine understanding
Motivated	Does not read for information; concentrates on decoding Can provide some details about selection Reading is initiated by teacher	Holds as much beginning information as possible and forgets the rest May describe what selection is about and provide some detail Reading is initiated by student	Identifies main idea; determines fact and non-fact Compares/ contrasts information with/ to other events and experiences Shares reading with others	Knows specific information he/she needs from text Develops questions unanswered by selection Actively seeks reading opportunities

Reading Rubric, Grade 5
(continued)

	Beginning	Developing	Capable	Expert
Strategic sorting	Differentiates fiction from nonfiction by structure of piece Can remember some of the important pieces	Can differentiate among structures used in fiction * Uses structure to assign order, remember characters, and identify problem/ goal	Can differentiate among nonfiction structures ** Uses structures to determine most important aspects of text to remember	Can articulate and analyze author's use of structure Discusses how structure assists reader in sorting important from unimportant
Asks questions	Does not have enough information to ask questions	Has difficulty asking questions	Can ask questions about what was read	Asks questions that tie this text to others
Self-correction strategies	Does not self-correct	Recognizes mistakes but has difficulty self-correcting	Has strategies for self-correction ***	Analyzes self-correction strategies as to best strategy ***
Identifies purpose	Has little understanding of reason for reading	Reads text because teacher said to	Establishes clear purpose for reading	Evaluates purpose for reading

    *   Fiction structures (examples): flashbacks, chronological, episodic, story within story
   ** Nonfiction structures (examples): topical, cause and effect, sequential, comparison/contrast, persuasive
 *** Self-correction or "fix-up" strategies: looks back, looks ahead, rereads, slows down, asks for help

Note. From *Meeting Standards & Raising Test Scores,* by R. K. Payne and D. S. Magee, 1999.

While this is an example of a reading rubric for fifth grade, it can be used with students in middle school (or high school) who are reading at a level below fifth grade. The indicators clearly identify performance level in the various categories for assessment.

SIXTH, SEVENTH, EIGHTH GRADES

PERSUASIVE FIRST DRAFT

1—Below expectations
2—Minimum
3—Mastery
4—Excellent

Words found in prompt: State your position, convince

OBJECTIVES	1	2	3	4
1. Stays on topic	Addresses topic/ purpose in skeletal or general manner Drifts from topic/ purpose (why to how-to) Information does not support position Responses are not persuasive	Addresses position and provides reasons Occasionally drifts from position/ reasons	Remains on topic Response is consistent Persuades adequately	Presents convincing reasons in logical, unified manner Persuades convincingly
2. Organization and structure	Lacks connection between responses Rambles and/or is repetitive Major gaps and inconsistencies	Has introduction and a conclusion Organization apparent Some gaps, rambling, and inconsistencies	Generally well organized and clear enough to understand reasons presented Transition from one thought to another Has introduction, body, and conclusion Gives at least three reasons in body paragraphs	Clear sense of order and completeness Effective use of transitional elements Consistent organizational strategy evident Has introduction, body, and conclusion Gives at least four reasons in body paragraphs
3. Language control	Brief phrases Sentence fragments Illogical, confusing sentences Repeated errors in spelling usage and word choice	Awkward or simple sentences Many errors in spelling, capitalization, and punctuation that do not affect understanding	Exhibits control of language Some grammatical errors interrupt flow of language Some variation in sentence structure Complete sentences	Consistent control of language Few, if any, grammatical errors Varied sentence construction, including compound and complex sentences

SIXTH, SEVENTH, EIGHTH GRADES

PERSUASIVE FIRST DRAFT
(continued)

OBJECTIVES	1	2	3	4
4. Support and elaboration	Insufficient elaboration to support position Brief list of nonspecific and unelaborated reasons Minimal word choice	Some elaboration and/or extension of reasons Number of specific reasons provided Limited word choice	Elaboration may support one fully developed reason or a lengthy set of less-developed ideas Effective word choice Exhibits at least two types of elaboration	Specific and well elaborated reasons that are clear and convincing Rich, unusual, and/or vivid word choice Exhibits three or more types of elaboration
5. Mechanics, grammar, and conventions	Major errors in capitalization, punctuation, and spelling Incomplete sentences	Some errors in capitalization, punctuation, and spelling Some mistakes in subject-verb agreement Some sentence fragments	Minor revisions in spelling, capitalization Punctuation needed Usually uses correct subject-verb agreement	Capitalization, punctuation, and spelling acceptable for publication Subject-verb agreement correct
Fluency *	0–100	100–150	150–250	250+

* These figures represent an approximate number of words occurring in papers with these scores; the focus, however, should be on elaborating ideas, not on counting words

Scoring for editing and revisions for final draft:

Score **only** the **final copy** of written compositions for mechanics, grammar, and conventions
Before scoring, students should edit and revise their first drafts for skills that have been taught

Note. From *Meeting Standards & Raising Test Scores,* by R. K. Payne and D. S. Magee, 1999.

Florida Comprehensive Assessment Test (FCAT) Mathematics

General Scoring Rubric for Short-Response (SR) Questions:
Grades 5, 8, and 10

2 points A score of two indicates that the student has demonstrated a thorough understanding of the mathematics concepts and/or procedures embodied in the task. The student has completed the task correctly, in a mathematically sound manner. When required, student explanations and/or interpretations are clear and complete. The response may contain minor flaws that do not detract from the demonstration of a thorough understanding.

1 point A score of one indicates that the student has provided a response that is only partially correct. For example, the student may provide a correct solution, but may demonstrate some misunderstanding of the underlying mathematical concepts or procedures. Conversely, a student may provide a computationally incorrect solution but could have applied appropriate and mathematically sound procedures, or the student's explanation could indicate an understanding of the task, despite the error.

0 points A score of zero indicates that the student has provided no response at all, or a completely incorrect or uninterpretable response, or demonstrated insufficient understanding of the mathematics concepts and/or procedures embodied in the task. For example, a student may provide some work that is mathematically correct, but the work does not demonstrate even a rudimentary understanding of the primary focus of the task.

Note. From Florida Department of Education, September 2004: http://fcat.fldoe.org/pdf/rubrcmat.pdf

General Scoring Rubric for Extended-Response (ER) Questions: Grades 5, 8, and 10

4 points A score of four is a response in which the student demonstrates a thorough understanding of the mathematics concepts and/or procedures embodied in the task. The student has responded correctly to the task, used mathematically sound procedures, and provided clear and complete explanations and interpretations. The response may contain minor flaws that do not detract from the demonstration of a thorough understanding.

3 points A score of three is a response in which the student demonstrates an understanding of the mathematics concepts and/or procedures embodied in the task. The student's response to the task is essentially correct, with the mathematical procedures used and the explanations and interpretations provided demonstrating an essential but less than thorough understanding. The response may contain minor flaws that reflect inattentive execution of mathematical procedures or indications of some misunderstanding of the underlying mathematics concepts and/or procedures.

2 points A score of two indicates that the student has demonstrated only a partial understanding of the mathematics concepts and/or procedures embodied in the task. Although the student may have used the correct approach to obtaining a solution or may have provided a correct solution, the student's work lacks an essential understanding of the underlying mathematical concepts. The response contains errors related to misunderstanding important aspects of the task, misuse of mathematical procedures, or faulty interpretations of results.

1 point A score of one indicates that the student has demonstrated a very limited understanding of the mathematics concepts and/or procedures embodied in the task. The student's response is incomplete and exhibits many flaws. Although the student's response has addressed some of the conditions of the task, the student reached an inadequate conclusion and/or provided reasoning that was faulty or incomplete. The response exhibits many flaws or may be incomplete.

0 points A score of zero indicates that the student has provided no response at all, or a completely incorrect or uninterpretable response, or demonstrated insufficient understanding of the mathematics concepts and/or procedures embodied in the task. For example, a student may provide some work that is mathematically correct, but the work does not demonstrate even a rudimentary understanding of the primary focus of the task.

Note. From Florida Department of Education, September 2004: http://fcat.fldoe.org/pdf/rubrcmat.pdf

Teacher and Student Artifacts Analysis:
A Tool to Analyze Quality of Assignments

EXAMPLES: Lesson plans, project guidelines, classroom guidelines/ procedures, rubrics, tests, homework assignments	**EXAMPLES:** Completed projects, research papers, tests, homework, writing samples, rubrics used for self-assessment, student notes
QUESTIONS TO ASK ABOUT ARTIFACTS	**QUESTIONS TO ASK ABOUT ARTIFACTS**
1. Is the process clearly identified (procedures, steps)?	1. Did the student complete the assignment?
2. Are student evaluation tools given (rubrics, grading guidelines, etc.)?	2. What was the level of difficulty of the assignment for the student?
3. Is the assignment relevant to the student in any way? (linked to a personal experience, a future story, a creative option)	3. Was the quality of the student work sufficient to assess student understanding of the task/content?
4. Is the purpose of the assignment to develop automaticity? If so, how much automaticity is required?	4. Was the finished project/assignment on grade level?
5. Is the assignment tied to grade-level standards and expectations?	5. Is the student able to demonstrate the use of the self-evaluation tool?
6. How often is the same kind of assignment given? Is there variation in the week?	6. Did the student follow the directions?
7. Does the assignment require thought?	
8. Is it a "beginning learning" assignment? If so, what are the opportunities to do the assignment with a peer or a group?	
9. Does it involve media/technology? If so, is that accessible to the student?	
10. Is the timeframe given to do the assignment reasonable for the majority of students?	
11. What is the motivation for the student? (tied to a future story, a work environment, a personal interest, an understanding of the content, the relationships with the teacher, personal expertise/ knowledge)	
12. Does the assignment provide any choice(s) for demonstrating understanding?	
13. To what extent is the assignment dependent on memory versus utilization of information sources?	

Note. From Engage and Graduate Your Secondary Students: Prevent Dropouts PowerPoint, 2009.

Analyzing assignments provides insight into the level of expectations for students. This matrix can be used to analyze teacher artifacts, as well as student artifacts. Ideally, this analysis is done in grade-level or department meetings; the focus is on the assignments (artifacts) and not on the individual who gave them. Such focus allows us to have a professional dialog without it becoming personal (product vs. person).

Activity

Choose an assignment that was recently given. Select three of the questions from the artifact analysis and analyze the assignment against those questions. Discuss with a colleague, explaining any changes you would make in the assignment.

Classroom Application

- Regular use of rubrics in content areas

- ELA teachers teach writing rubric to entire staff

- Open-response rubric consistent in all core subject areas

U R TOPS, a strategy for open-response questions, was included in Process 1.

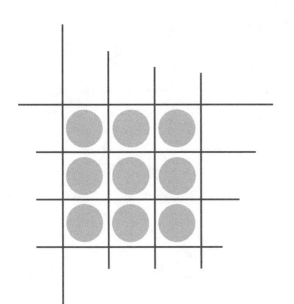

Process 9:
Voice, Putting
Students in Charge of
Their Own Learning,
Relational Learning

Why Voice, Putting Students in Charge of Their Own Learning, Relational Learning

- Understand and appropriately use the three voices of an individual

- Assist students in taking ownership of their own learning

- Build relationships of mutual respect

Benefits to Teachers

- Use of the adult voice in interactions with students minimizes and defuses conflict

- Knowing the voice called for by the situation can help the teacher be more successful in his/her interactions with students

- Teachers who help students plan for their own learning assist them in being more self-directed and developing a positive future story; this can increase their motivation and interest in school

- When relationships of mutual respect exist between teacher and student, a more positive climate is built in the classroom

Voices

CHILD

- Quit picking on me.
- You don't love me.
- You want me to leave.
- It's your fault.
- Don't blame me.
- He/she did it.
- You make me mad.
- You made me do it.

PARENT

- You (shouldn't) should do that.
- It's wrong (right) to do _____.
- That's stupid, immature, out of line, ridiculous.
- Life's not fair. Get busy.
- You are good, bad, worthless, beautiful (any judgmental, evaluative comment).
- You do as I say.
- If you weren't so _____, this wouldn't happen to you.
- Why can't you be like _____?

ADULT

- In what ways could this be resolved?
- I would like to recommend _____.
- What are choices in this situation?
- I am comfortable (uncomfortable) with _____.
- Options that could be considered are _____.
- For me to be comfortable, I need the following things to occur: _____.
- These are the consequences of that choice/action: _____.
- We agree to disagree.

Note. Adapted from work of Eric Berne, 1996.

While most individuals have three voices inside their head, students who had to parent themselves from an early age often lack the adult voice. It is the adult voice that provides for negotiation and enables one to deal with issues without feeling threatened. This is the voice that often needs to be developed with young people. It is this voice that also builds relationships of mutual respect, while the parent voice is used to stop a behavior that could be harmful to oneself or others (Payne, 2005). For more information on voices, see Payne's *A Framework for Understanding Poverty.*

Discipline Referrals

1. Ninety percent come from 10% of the students.

2. Ninety-five percent occur in the first or last five minutes of class time.

3. Eighty percent come from 11% of the staff.

Note. From Meeting Standards & Raising Test Scores PowerPoint, by R. K. Payne and D. S. Magee, 2005.

Of these referrals, what percentage would you estimate are related to issues of language and voice? Why do 95% of referrals come from the first or last five minutes of class?

Student Accountability for Learning

Questions I got right and could get right again	Questions I did or did not do correctly but am not sure how to do	Questions where I had no clue
1, 3, 4, 5, 9, 11, 14, 15, 19	2, 6, 7, 12, 13, 18, 20	8, 10, 16, 17

Note. Developed by Shelley Rex.

According to Scherer (2008), ownership is more powerful for today's students than outside accountability measures. In addressing this ownership, she cites a study by the Center for Public Education (2008) that notes the importance of small learning communities. Collegial relationships among staff, as well as more personalized learning for students, are supported through these smaller communities. This will receive further attention in the upcoming section on relational learning.

Differentiation of instruction, which is emphasized so much today, is also a way for students to be accountable for their learning, according to Tomlinson (2008). Such instruction also helps students "form their own identities as learners" (p. 26).

This grid is used by students when taking an assessment. In the first box, they list the questions they are confident they got correct. In the second, they list the questions they did or did not do correctly but also were not sure how to do. The last box lists the questions they had no idea as to how to do. As they work back through the questions and identify specific strategies they can use on the objectives/concepts being assessed by the question, they determine which ones can be moved to one of the other boxes. They then are able to count the number of questions they thought they got right and compare this to the number needed to pass.

Completed Chart After Interventions/Reteaching

Questions I got right and could get right again	Questions I did or did not do correctly but am not sure how to do	Questions where I had no clue
1, 3, 4, 5, 9, 11, 14, 15, 19	2, 6, 7, 12, 13, 18, 20	8, 10, 16, 17
2, 6, 7, 8, 10, 13, 17, 18		

Note. Developed by Shelley Rex.

This is an example of the modified grid once students worked through the questions a second time. This process provides students a way to take greater ownership in their learning.

Relational Learning Has Seven Characteristics

1. Relationships of mutual respect with teachers and administrators

2. A peer group to belong to that is positive and not destructive

3. A coach or advocate who helps the student

4. If not a member of the dominant culture, the student has access to individuals (or histories of individuals) who have attained success and retained connections to their roots

5. Bridging social capital (e-mail buddies, mentors, et al.) to the larger society

6. At the secondary school level, a very specific and clear plan for addressing his/her own learning performance

7. A safe environment (emotionally, verbally, and physically)

Note. From *Under-Resourced Learners* (pp. 20–21), by R. K. Payne, 2008.

Characteristics 1–5 all contribute to the personalized learning environment referenced in the study for the Center for Public Education.

Relational Learning

Action steps that communicate an appropriate level of guidance and structure:

1. Know something about each student

2. Engage in behaviors that indicate affection for each student

3. Bring student interests into content—and personalize learning activities

4. Engage in physical behaviors that communicate interest in students

5. Use humor when appropriate

6. Consistently enforce positive and negative consequences

7. Project a sense of emotional objectivity

8. Maintain a cool exterior

Note. From *The Art and Science of Teaching* (pp. 154–161), by R. J. Marzano, 2007.

In working with today's Gen Y students, technology must be integrated into lessons. Beyond the use of technology in the classroom, teachers may want to consider social web technologies. Richardson (2008) says, "One of the biggest challenges educators face right now is figuring out how to help students create, navigate, and grow the powerful, individualized networks of learning that bloom on the Web and helping them do this effectively, ethically, and safely" (pp. 17–18). As teachers do this, there is also the opportunity for them to practice relational learning through the posting of their own blogs or even utilizing a wiki in their classroom.

Relational Learning: Techniques for Secondary Students

1. At the beginning of the year, tell students about yourself, your credentials, and what you hope they learn during the year. Then ask them to write back to you and tell you things that would help you teach them. Do they work after school? What do they like about school? What do they hate? What helps them learn? Etc.

2. One high school teacher gave an independent assignment every Friday. He called students up to his desk one at a time, went over their grades with them, and asked if there was anything he could do to help them with the class. Behavior improved tremendously because now there was a relationship between the teacher and students.

To integrate technology, e-mailing responses to the questions in No. 1 (above) can increase students' interest and motivation in responding. As described in No. 2, students also are taking more accountability for their learning while the relationship improves.

How Do You Build Relationships of Mutual Respect?

Students look for three things:

- Insistence

- Support

- High expectations (not unreasonable—but high)

Issue	Evidenced	Needed	Not Applicable
Teacher calls students by name.			
Teacher uses courtesies: "please," "thank you," etc.			
Students use courtesies with each other and with teacher.			
Teacher calls on all students.			
Teacher gets into proximity (within an arm's reach) of all students—daily if possible, but at least weekly.			
Teacher greets students at door.			
Teacher smiles at students.			
Classroom has businesslike atmosphere.			
Students are given tools to assess/evaluate own work.			
Student-generated questions are used as part of instruction.			
Grading/scoring is clear and easily understood.			
Students may ask for extra help from teacher.			

Note. From *Under-Resourced Learners* (p. 22), by R. K. Payne, 2008.

Use this rubric to assess yourself on building relationships of mutual respect with students. Also, give this rubric to students and ask them how they would modify it, then adapt it accordingly, as appropriate.

Activity

For one student, briefly outline a plan for building a relationship of mutual respect and helping him/her take accountability for his/her own learning.

Classroom Application

- Monitor for use of adult voice in the classroom

- Do data conferencing with students

- Monitor for examples of relational learning

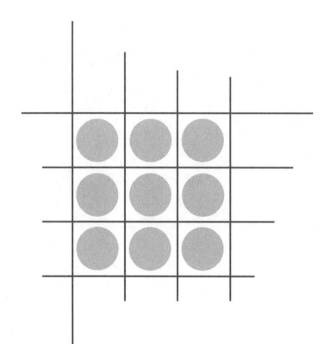

Appendix

Implementation

Implementing the Model at the Elementary School Level

At the elementary level, these processes can be taught to individual grade-level teachers or multiple grade levels in a session. We refer to these sessions as technical assistance. The key is that groups be small enough to receive the individual attention that will enhance teachers' professional growth and learning and allow the group to move quickly through the processes. Roving substitutes can be provided for classrooms if professional development days are limited. The substitute teachers would move throughout the building to cover classes while teachers are released for two hours of job-embedded professional development.

Implementing the Model at the Secondary School Level

At the secondary level, technical assistance is provided to teachers through content or department areas. However, if there are so many teachers within a department that the progress of the group could be impeded by the sheer number of teachers, technical assistance could be done by course. And while all content areas are important in providing world-class education for our students, this model emphasizes literacy and math skills, as these are critical to all other areas. The intent is not to exclude any content or department area, but to emphasize math and literacy development within the other departments. Again, roving substitutes could be provided to allow release time for teachers to meet and to collaborate on the processes and their strategy-based applications.

Model Alternative

An alternative to the model, especially in larger schools, is for the technical assistant to work with the principal and leadership team, provided there is a cross-representation of departments involved on the leadership team.

Implementing the Model with or Without External Technical Assistance

A campus trained in the foundational trainings and the optional Meeting AYP training may be able to implement the model without external assistance if it has strong leadership and curriculum/instructional specialists to work with teachers. However, our experience has been that most campuses find more success with the model by first utilizing aha! Process consultants to provide the technical assistance. Having leaders or campus-based specialists "shadow" the consultant during the technical assistance is encouraged, as follow-up between consultant visits will be focused on implementation and the model itself.

Sustaining the Model

Working in small groups by grade level or department simulates professional learning communities. The importance of the dialog and support that teachers find in these settings cannot be overstated. With the aha! Process model, continuous improvement is ongoing as teachers work to refine the processes from year to year, always focusing on the data of the current students whom they are teaching. Refining assessments and analyzing data become easier over the years because teachers are utilizing processes. As they work with, adapt, and understand the processes at a deeper level, their professional practice and what they spend time on changes: They begin spending more time on that which yields a payoff and strong results. This model is neither a prescription nor a program; instead it builds capacity and focuses on the sharing of best practices. Building on the positive educational practices already in place on the campus, the climate and culture of a building will increasingly shift to greater student learning and achievement as processes are implemented and the staff sees student achievement rise. Finally, schools working with the model are encouraged to send staff to trainer certification workshops so that they can provide the foundational trainings when teacher turnover occurs.

Administrator Checklist
Gridding Student Data/Targeted Students

ADMINISTRATIVE EXPECTATIONS	Date Completed
Set date for staff meeting to grid student data, as near to start of school as possible	
Week before meeting:	
Gather all state test reports for students currently served in building, including overall results by grade level/content area that show student performance by standard and individual student scores	
If state reports do not identify students by ethnicity, free/reduced lunch, disability, and LEP, gather these lists	
Prepare data grid template	
Make appropriate number of copies of reports, lists, and templates for staff use	
Include written reminder of upcoming meeting to grid data in school notes, office memos, faculty meetings, faculty message board, faculty announcements, and/or faculty e-mails; remind teachers to bring their student rosters to meeting	
Identify student performance "cut" scores	
Identify AYP targets from previous year and current year	
During meeting:	
Identify student subgroups and place on data grid template	
Identify performance categories and "cut" scores and place on data grid (note that "cut" scores may vary by performance category and/or grade level)	
Review process for gridding data	
Allow teachers ample time to grid at least one class set of data	
After a grade level/content area completes one grid, work staff through compilation of grade-level profile (number of students by subgroup and performance category are counted, and this number is placed on profile sheet)	
Determine AYP status from profile sheet	
Establish performance goals based on current data/AYP	
After meeting:	
Provide time and expectation that teachers will complete data grids for each class period	
Set date for completion of all grids; have grids submitted to _____ (teachers should keep one copy for their records)	
Set date for individual teacher/grade-level/department/principal conferences to discuss patterns, strengths, concerns, etc., noted on grids	
Conduct conferences/meetings	
During conferences/meetings (see Checklists: Data Analysis/Targeted Students, and Data Analysis/Target Standards):	
Identify targeted students	
Identify interventions for targeted students	
Identify target standards	
Establish plan to address target standards	

Administrator Checklist
Data Analysis/Targeted Students

ADMINISTRATIVE EXPECTATIONS	Date Completed
After teachers have gridded data, set date for grade-level or department meetings/conferences to discuss student data (as near to start of school as possible)	
Week before meeting:	
Include written reminder of upcoming meetings to discuss data in school notes, office memos, faculty meetings, faculty message board, faculty announcements, and/or faculty e-mails	
During meeting:	
Using data grids, identify patterns that are evident related to subgroups	
Identify students who are in more than one subgroup and discuss implications	
Identify which students missed passing by slim margin	
Identify which students passed by slim margin	
Analyze individual students in each testing band and decide which students can be moved to next performance band based on specific interventions	
Complete resource analysis on selected students to help determine types of interventions that might be most successful with those students	
Determine other interventions needed and establish plan	
After meeting:	
Monitor progress of identified students during quarterly grade-level/ department meetings (analyze grades, attendance, behavior)	
Upon receipt of state test results, identify whether student performance improved	

TARGETED STUDENTS

TEACHER _____ CLASS _____

1. List students by name
2. Record date progress was monitored
3. Indicate whether student improved score on state assessment

STUDENT NAME	First-Quarter Score	Second-Quarter Score	Third-Quarter Score	Fourth-Quarter Score	Did Student Improve Score on State Assessment?

Administrator Checklist
Data Analysis/Target Standards

ADMINISTRATIVE EXPECTATIONS	Date Completed
After teachers have gridded data, set date for grade-level or department meetings/conferences to discuss student data (as near to start of school as possible); may want to combine with meeting to analyze targeted students	
Week before meeting:	
Include written reminder of upcoming meetings to discuss data in school notes, office memos, faculty meetings, faculty message board, faculty announcements, and/or faculty e-mails	
During meeting:	
Analyze student performance on each standard tested, noting percentages of students who met standard or didn't meet standard	
Identify areas of concern by grade level/content area	
Identify areas of strength by grade level/content area	
Identify factors that could have contributed to low/high student performance on each standard—e.g., use of or lack of step sheet, mental models, time when standard was taught, lack of content-specific vocabulary, etc.	
Identify plan to improve performance on weak standards and increase or sustain performance on others	
Revise time and content grids, if necessary	
Collect copies of revised time and content grids	
Collect copies of action plan to improve performance	
After meeting:	
Monitor implementation of action plan and progress toward target standards during quarterly grade-level/department time and content meetings	

TARGET STANDARDS

TEACHER _____   CLASS/GRADE _____

AREAS OF STRENGTH	AREAS OF CONCERN	PLAN TO ADDRESS CONCERN

Administrator Checklist
Monitoring Instruction and Behavior via Walk-Throughs

ADMINISTRATIVE EXPECTATIONS	Date Completed
In staff meeting, discuss plan and expectations for administrative walk-throughs and for providing feedback to teachers	
Include written reminder of these expectations in school notes, office memos, faculty meetings, faculty message board, faculty announcements, and/or faculty e-mails	
Prior to starting walk-through process:	
Identify teachers needing immediate support and feedback	
Have secretary or administrative assistant add teachers' names to attached roster	
Block time on calendar to complete walk-throughs weekly	
Decide which walk-through rubrics will be utilized	
Conduct walk-throughs	
After walk-throughs have been completed:	
Provide feedback to teachers through e-mail or written communication	
Schedule conference with teachers when concerns are more appropriately addressed through face-to-face meetings	
Establish plan to revisit teachers needing additional support	
Provide monthly report to supervisor regarding walk-through process—i.e., numbers of walk-throughs completed, patterns noted, areas of strength, areas of concern, etc.	

TEACHER ROSTER

Teacher Name	Date/ Class Period	Date/ Class Period	Date/ Class Period	Date/ Class Period	Date/ Class Period	Date/ Class Period	Date/ Class Period	Date/ Class Period	Date/ Class Period	Date/ Class Period

Administrator Checklist
Time and Content Grids

ADMINISTRATIVE EXPECTATIONS	First Quarter	Second Quarter	Third Quarter	Fourth Quarter
Week before meeting:				
Communicate meeting date to teachers through school notes, office memos, faculty meetings, faculty message board, faculty announcements, and/or faculty e-mails				
Communicate that following materials are needed for meeting: curriculum guide, scope and sequence, pacing guide, curriculum frameworks, and any other curriculum-related documents from state website and textbooks/teacher editions				
During meeting:				
Review steps to grid time and content (process 2, Meeting AYP with 5 Simple Processes training)				
Work with teachers to complete first-quarter grids for each content area (at elementary level, focus on math and reading; choose content area with lowest student performance)				
Obtain for your administrative files hard copies or electronic copies of grids with first quarter completed				
Determine plan for completing remaining quarters of grid				
Set date that completed time and content grids will be submitted to administrator				
After meeting:				
Check lesson plans against time and content grids				
Do walk-throughs of classes to monitor adherence to time and content grids				
Schedule quarterly grade-level/department meetings to discuss instruction and pacing per time and content grids				
During subsequent meeting:				
Require teachers to explain how they are using time and content grids to plan instruction, "where they are" in instruction per grids, what is working/what is not working (if teacher is not following grid, private conference should be conducted after meeting)				
If grid needs to be modified, entire grade level must come to consensus before making change				
After receiving state test results:				
Schedule meeting to identify areas of strengths and weaknesses in student performance and compare with time and content grids				
Subsequent years:				
After teachers have disaggregated student test data for their current group of students, schedule meeting to identify strengths and weaknesses—and modify time and content grids to address these (may include changing amount of time needed to teach concept, time when concept is taught, etc.)				

Administrator Checklist
Time and Content Grids

Date _____

ADMINISTRATIVE EXPECTATIONS	Completed	Not Completed	N/A
Review time and content grids			
Spot-check teacher lesson plans against time and content grids			
Use time and content grids for walk-through observations			
Conference with teachers about time and content grids, lesson plans, and walk-through observations			
Use time and content grids to conference with teachers about benchmark assessment data			

Administrator Checklist
Ten-Question Test/Quarterly Benchmark Test

Subject: _____

ADMINISTRATIVE EXPECTATIONS	First Quarter	Second Quarter	Third Quarter	Fourth Quarter
Week before testing window:				
Place 10-question testing window on school calendar				
Include written reminder of upcoming quarterly/10-question test in school notes, office memos, faculty meetings, faculty message board, faculty announcements, and/or faculty e-mails				
Obtain for your administrative files hard copies or electronic copies of quarterly assessment				
Require teachers to include testing days in their class lesson plans				
During testing window:				
Walk-through classes to monitor that tests are being administered				
Include testing tips/hidden rules of test taking in morning school announcements				
Following testing:				
Require that teachers grade tests				
Require teachers to complete student and item analysis for each class and provide principal/assistant principal with copy by specified date (attached)				
Require teachers to complete longitudinal record of student quarterly assessment grades and provide principal/assistant principal with copy by specified date (attached)				
Schedule meeting with teachers (by grade level or department) to discuss results of test				
During meeting:				
Identify standards that need to be retaught and plan for reteaching, including how and when				
Identify students who need immediate intervention and determine intervention(s)				
Establish plan to monitor whether intervention is working; what will you expect to happen if intervention is working?				
Set date for follow-up meeting in three weeks to monitor progress; at follow-up meeting, continue or modify intervention				
To monitor progress, set date for another follow-up meeting six weeks after intervention was put in place				

Subject: _____

TEACHER _____ **CLASS** _____

1. List students by name
2. Record their quarterly assessment score

STUDENT NAME	First-Quarter Score	Second-Quarter Score	Third-Quarter Score	Fourth-Quarter Score	Average

TEACHER _____ **CLASS** _____ **1 2 3 4 Quarter** (circle)

1. List students
2. Label table with standard number that matches each test question
3. Mark items that student missed
4. Copy and return copy to _____ on _____

Student Name	Item	1	2	3	4	5	6	7	8	9	10	11	Average
	Standard #												
Total % Missed													

Administrator Checklist
Monitoring Implementation of Mental Models

ADMINISTRATIVE EXPECTATIONS	Date Completed
Schedule faculty meeting to allow grade-level/department leaders to share mental models with entire staff	
Include written reminder of schoolwide faculty meeting to share strategies in school notes, office memos, faculty meetings, faculty message board, faculty announcements, and/or faculty e-mails	
Facilitate faculty meeting	
Before walk-throughs begin:	
Include written reminder of administrative plan to complete walk-throughs to monitor implementation of mental models in school notes, office memos, faculty meetings, faculty message board, faculty announcements, and/or faculty e-mails	
Create staff roster to monitor walk-throughs	
Identify teachers who would benefit most from administrative feedback	
Block time on personal calendar to conduct walk-throughs	
During walk-throughs:	
Complete appropriate walk-through form	
After walk-throughs:	
Provide completed walk-through form to teacher	
Meet individually with teacher if areas of concern are observed during walk-through	
For those teachers requiring a conference, visit classroom again within one week to monitor progress	
If progress is not made, develop additional plan of support collaboratively with teacher and continue to monitor	

TEACHER ROSTER

Teacher Name	Date/ Class Period	Date/ Class Period	Date/ Class Period	Date/ Class Period	Date/ Class Period	Date/ Class Period	Date/ Class Period	Date/ Class Period	Date/ Class Period	Date/ Class Period

Administrator Checklist
Interventions

ADMINISTRATIVE EXPECTATIONS	Date Completed	Date Completed	Date Completed	Date Completed
Schedule meeting with campus leadership team to identify departmental and campuswide interventions				
One week prior to meeting:				
Include written reminder of upcoming meeting in school notes, office memos, faculty meetings, faculty message board, faculty announcements, and/or faculty e-mails				
During meeting:				
Facilitate meeting with leadership team to identify available interventions and other needed interventions				
If additional interventions are needed, establish plan to provide them				
Establish plan to communicate interventions to other staff and to identify students needing interventions				
Establish plan to monitor whether intervention is working; what will you expect to happen if intervention is working?				
After meeting:				
Attend meetings of grade levels/ departments to develop intervention plans for individual students (Student Intervention sheet attached)				
Set date for follow-up meeting in three weeks to monitor progress; at follow-up meeting, continue or modify intervention				
To monitor progress, set date for another follow-up meeting six weeks after intervention was put in place				
Repeat three steps above every quarter				
At end of year:				
Meet with leadership team to evaluate impact of interventions and plan for coming year				

Student Intervention Plan Sheet

Student_____

RDG   MATH   OTHER
SES   SPED   LEP

	STANDARDS BEING ADDRESSED						
Proficiency Goal							
Performance Level							
Interventions				Date Started		Date Ended	
Responsible Party							
Evaluation							

Note. Developed by Shelley Rex.

Administrator Checklist
Monitoring Grades

ADMINISTRATIVE EXPECTATIONS	Date Completed
Set date for grade-level/department meetings to analyze grades from each quarter	
Week before meeting:	
Include written reminder of upcoming meeting to analyze grades in school notes, office memo, faculty meeting, faculty message board, faculty announcements, and/or faculty e-mail	
During meeting:	
Teachers complete grade-distribution chart by identifying number of A's, B's, C's, D's, and F's (or numerical equivalents) given during quarter for each course/subject they teach	
By individual teacher and grade level/department, identify number of students who made A's	
By individual teacher and grade level/department, identify number of students who made D's and F's	
Discuss grades of targeted students	
How do numbers of A's, D's, and F's compare with state assessment percentages?	
Identify factors contributing to student failures	
Discuss implications of students' grades with regard to success on state assessments	
Identify individual students who need student/teacher conference and establish timeline for meeting with them (work with students to set improvement goals)	
Complete resource analysis on these students to help determine types of interventions that might be most successful with them	
After meeting:	
Monitor teacher/student conferences and improvement plans; chart student progress (based on grades) each quarter	
Meet with individual teachers who have an unusually high number of failures	

TARGETED STUDENTS

TEACHER _____ **CLASS** _____

1. List students by name
2. Record date progress was monitored
3. Indicate whether student improved score on state assessment

STUDENT NAME	First-Quarter Score	Second-Quarter Score	Third-Quarter Score	Fourth-Quarter Score	Did Student Improve Score on State Assessment?

Administrator Checklist
Monitoring Implementation of Step Sheets

ADMINISTRATIVE EXPECTATIONS	Date Completed
In faculty meeting, lead discussion on purpose of step sheets (teacher-created and student-created) and expected use of the strategy	
Before walk-throughs begin:	
Include written reminder of administrative plan to complete walk-throughs to monitor implementation of step sheets in school notes, office memos, faculty meetings, faculty message board, faculty announcements, and/or faculty e-mails	
Create staff roster to monitor walk-throughs	
Identify teachers who would benefit most from administrative feedback	
Block time on personal calendar to conduct walk-throughs	
During walk-throughs:	
Complete appropriate walk-through form	
After walk-throughs:	
Provide completed walk-through form to teacher	
Meet individually with teacher if areas of concern are observed during walk-through	
For those teachers requiring a conference, visit classroom again within one week to monitor progress	
If progress is not made, develop additional plan of support collaboratively with teacher and continue to monitor	

TEACHER ROSTER

Teacher Name	Date/ Class Period	Date/ Class Period	Date/ Class Period	Date/ Class Period	Date/ Class Period	Date/ Class Period	Date/ Class Period	Date/ Class Period	Date/ Class Period	Date/ Class Period

Administrator Checklist
Monitoring Implementation of Plan and Label

ADMINISTRATIVE EXPECTATIONS	Date Completed
Schedule faculty meeting to allow grade-level/department leaders to share plan and label for text and math problem-solving strategy with entire staff	
Include written reminder of schoolwide faculty meeting to share strategies in school notes, office memos, faculty meetings, faculty message board, faculty announcements, and/or faculty e-mails	
Facilitate faculty meeting	
Before walk-throughs begin:	
Include written reminder of administrative plan to complete walk-throughs to monitor implementation of plan and label strategy in school notes, office memos, faculty meetings, faculty message board, faculty announcements, and/or faculty e-mails	
Create staff roster to monitor walk-throughs	
Identify teachers who would benefit most from administrative feedback	
Block time on personal calendar to conduct walk-throughs	
During walk-throughs:	
Complete appropriate walk-through form	
After walk-throughs:	
Provide completed walk-through form to teacher	
Meet individually with teacher if areas of concern are observed during walk-through	
For those teachers requiring a conference, visit classroom again within one week to monitor progress	
If progress is not made, develop additional plan of support collaboratively with teacher and continue to monitor	

TEACHER ROSTER

Teacher Name	Date/ Class Period	Date/ Class Period	Date/ Class Period	Date/ Class Period	Date/ Class Period	Date/ Class Period	Date/ Class Period	Date/ Class Period	Date/ Class Period	Date/ Class Period

Administrator Checklist
Monitoring Student Question Making

ADMINISTRATIVE EXPECTATIONS	First Quarter	Second Quarter	Third Quarter	Fourth Quarter
Schedule grade-level/department meetings to discuss purpose of student question making; with teachers, develop step sheet for teaching question making to students (use *Research-Based Strategies* book, Strategy 4)		X	X	X
Include written reminder of student question making expectation in school notes, office memos, faculty meetings, faculty message board, faculty announcements, and/or faculty e-mails				
In grade-level/department meetings, review student work samples that contain student-generated questions				
Solicit feedback from teachers regarding strengths and challenges of using the strategy				
Identify ways to help teachers address challenges of using the strategy				

Administrator Checklist
Monitoring Implementation of State Rubrics

ADMINISTRATIVE EXPECTATIONS	Date Completed
Schedule grade-level/department meeting with English/language arts teachers (and math or other departments, if applicable) to discuss state rubric(s) used for writing assessments and/or open response items	
With department (1) review rubric's expectations, (2) discuss use of rubric at all grade levels within department by teachers, (3) discuss direct instruction to students regarding rubric's expectations, and (4) outline plan of anticipated use of rubric at each grade level	
Schedule faculty meeting to allow grade-level/department leaders to share rubric(s) with entire staff; identify staff members who will lead presentation and provide support as they plan their presentation	
Include written reminder of schoolwide faculty meeting to share rubrics in school notes, office memos, faculty meetings, faculty message board, faculty announcements, and/or faculty e-mails	
Facilitate faculty meeting	
Schedule meetings with each grade level/department to outline expectations for writing assignments/open-response items and use of rubric(s) for assessing these	
If needed, outline plan to provide follow-up support for teachers who are hesitant or uncomfortable with writing assignments and use of rubric	
Monitor use of rubric(s) and writing and/or expectations regarding open-response items	

Administrator Checklist
Implementation of Testing Strategies

ADMINISTRATIVE EXPECTATIONS	Date Completed
Schedule meeting with campus leadership team to identify campuswide testing strategies for use in classroom and on state assessment	
One week before meeting:	
Include written reminder of upcoming meeting in school notes, office memos, faculty meetings, faculty message board, faculty announcements, and/or faculty e-mails	
During meeting:	
Identify input strategies needed for student success on state assessment	
Brainstorm list of observable student testing behaviors and expectations	
Reach consensus on list of 5–10 behaviors	
Identify steps needed to implement the testing processes in classroom, then utilize with students; include student incentives	
Identify when implementation will begin and ways to determine that testing strategies are used in classrooms prior to test	
Identify how and when testing expectations will be communicated to entire faculty; identify staff members who will lead presentation, and provide support as they plan their presentation	
After meeting:	
Schedule faculty meeting to allow members of leadership team to share strategies with entire staff	
Include written reminder of schoolwide faculty meeting to share strategies in school notes, office memos, faculty meetings, faculty message board, faculty announcements, and/or faculty e-mails	
Facilitate faculty meeting	
Monitor use of strategies	

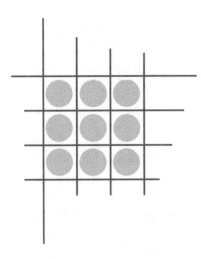

References

Berne, E. (1996). *Games people play: The basic handbook of transactional analysis.* New York, NY: Ballantine Books.

Bloom, B. S., Englehart, M. D., Furst, E. J., Hill, W. H., & Krathwohl, D. R. (1956). *Taxonomy of educational objectives: The classification of goals: Handbook I: Cognitive domain.* New York, NY: David McKay.

Center for Public Education. (2008). *Full report on the effects of school organization on student engagement.* Alexandria, VA.

Comer, J. (1995). Lecture given at Education Service Center, Region IV. Houston, TX.

Cooper, S., & Gargan, A. (2009, September). Rubrics in education: Old term, new meanings. *Kappan, 91*(1), 54–55.

Ellis, K. D. (2004). *Putting the pieces together.* Highlands, TX: aha! Process.

Florida Department of Education. (2004, September). http://fcat.fldoe.org/pdf/rubrcmat.pdf

Hollingsworth, J., & Ybarra, S. (2000). Analyzing classroom instruction: Curriculum calibration.http://www.dataworks-ed.com/ and http://pubs.cde.ca.gov/tcsii/documentlibrary/curiclumcalbration.asp

Guskey, T. (2003, February). How classroom assessments improve learning. *Educational Leadership, 60*(5), 6–11.

Marzano, R. J. (2007). *The art and science of teaching: A comprehensive framework for effective instruction.* Alexandria, VA: Association for Supervision and Curriculum Development.

Mental models for English/language arts: Grades 1–6. (2007). Highlands, TX: aha! Process.

Mental models for math: Grades 6–12. (2006). Highlands, TX: aha! Process.

Payne, R. K. (2002). *Understanding learning: The how, the why, the what.* Highlands, TX: aha! Process.

Payne, R. K. (2005). *A framework for understanding poverty* (5th ed.). Highlands, TX: aha! Process.

Payne, R. K. (2005). *Learning structures* (3rd ed.). Highlands, TX: aha! Process.

Payne, R. K. (2008). *Under-resourced learners: 8 strategies to boost student achievement.* Highlands, TX: aha! Process.

Payne, R. K. (2009). *Research-based strategies: Narrowing the achievement gap for under-resourced students.* Highlands, TX: aha! Process.

Payne, R. K. (2009). Engage and graduate your students: Prevent dropouts workshop handouts. Highlands, TX: aha! Process.

Payne, R. K., & Magee, D. S. (1999). *Meeting standards & raising test scores—When you don't have much time or money.* Highlands, TX: aha! Process.

Payne, R. K., & Magee, D. S. (2005). Meeting standards & raising test scores—When you don't have much time or money PowerPoint. Highlands, TX: aha! Process.

Richardson, W. (2008, November). Footprints in the digital age. *Educational Leadership, 66*(3), 16–19.

Ronka, D., Lachat, M., Slaughter, R., & Meltzer, J. (2008, December/2009, January). Answering the questions that count. *Educational Leadership, 66*(4), 18–24.

Scherer, M. (2008, November). Learning: Whose job is it? *Educational Leadership, 66*(3), 7.

Tomlinson, C. A. (2008, November). The goals of differentiation. *Educational Leadership, 66*(3), 26–30.

Wisconsin Department of Public Instruction. (2009). http://www.dpi.state.wi.us/

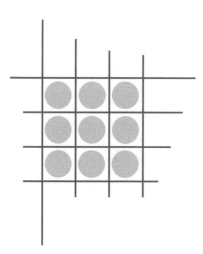

About the Authors

Ruby K. Payne, Ph.D., is a career educator, administrator, consultant, and founder of aha! Process, Inc. Her trailblazing efforts to address the needs of under-resourced learners include dozens of publications and training programs that have served hundreds of thousands of educators at all levels. Dr. Payne's landmark book, *A Framework for Understanding Poverty,* has sold more than 1 million copies, and her collaboration with other educators has touched countless lives with practical, proven strategies for helping students succeed.

Donna S. Magee, Ed.D., is a professional educator with 30 years of experience in all aspects of public education: teacher, principal, administrator, and consultant. Dr. Magee's understanding of school leadership, collaboration, and systemic change interfaces seamlessly with Dr. Ruby Payne's work on poverty. These skills enhance her work with schools and districts in outlining and implementing training initiatives designed to embed the School Improvement Model into their systems.